I0627057

Solivagant

Steps for Solo Travel Around the World

Hannah Marie.

Copyright © 2024 Hannah Marie.

All rights reserved.

Solivagant
from Latin

so·liv·a·gant, pronounced sō′livəgənt

(n.) a solitary wanderer
(adj.) rambling alone: marked by solitary wandering

For all of those who have encouraged me along my journey:
Thank you for keeping me grounded.

This Guidebook Contains:

Introduction

This little handbook is for those who have a strong desire to travel. If you have ever thought about traveling to another country, but don't know quite where to start, you've come to the right place! You picked up this book for a reason. Maybe you are glancing at it because the cover caught your eye, which motivates you to join me in my travel adventures around the world. Another reason could be because you have always wanted to travel, but are a little intimidated by the thought of going at it alone. You might have always been fascinated by friends who travel the world but have no clue where to start. Have you ever thought, *There are too many factors to traveling alone that makes it nearly impossible to plan anything beyond a short road trip*?

If any of this applies to you, this little book is exactly what you need! These are excuses that you tell yourself because traveling around by yourself seems too difficult. There are too many steps and too many variables. Let me tell you a little secret. Yes, there are several steps and oh, so many variables! But if you know what to expect, the situations that you land in won't seem so strange. The sections in this book are your own personal stepping stones! I've written a practical guide to push you out of your comfort zone and into something new. It shows some of the main steps that you need to get you out of the house and to explore the world around you, even if you are venturing out alone. It doesn't have to be a scary experience; travel is a grand adventure!

When I started traveling, I did not expect to love it as much as I do. In this book I lay out basic steps on what to expect, how to plan, and personal stories from my own travel adventures. I explain things from the perspective of an American in the States, but hope that this touches people in all corners of the globe; anyone ready to see the world! Let's find one adventure at a time! While most of the information in this book is geared towards traveling to other countries around the world, Chapter Five is specific to gallivanting within the United States. I have the unique experience of having already set out alone on many explorations and will take you with me on this virtual one, explaining how to prepare, what to look out for, and how to gain the most from your travel experiences. I've visited over fourteen countries outside of the United States, not including multiple visits to England, Holland, Mexico, Nicaragua, and Peru. I also include some favorite visits around the States and Canada, for those who prefer to stay close to home during their treks.

Until writing this book, I had a full-time teaching job, maintained a "normal" lifestyle and still traveled sometimes with friends and immediate family. I have no spouse or children of my own yet, but include kid-friendly suggestions, favorite inspirational travel books in the References, and also helpful tips and blogs from travelers who have varying disabilities. Don't let your excuses stop you from expanding your view of the world! The reasons you have not traveled much are probably legitimate, but there is a method to travel that you can learn here! Each section of the book is tailored to lead every step of the way when traveling solo, like a detailed checklist. It encourages you to get out and explore, not just dream about it for the next ten years.

The chapter layout is similar to a bullet journal, including fun doodles throughout, inspired by my own travels. The physical book is small enough that it can be carried on your adventures as you reach new destinations. I have also included some language tips and favorite phrase books in the References because part of getting to know a culture is finding ways to be respectful. When practicing a language, I personally prefer Pimsleur, a conversational language app, but also use Duolingo regularly to learn basic vocabulary. Several of the books in References are not written by professionals, but are chronicled memoirs from those who choose to wander off the beaten path to discover a little more about other countries and cultures. One day, it might be you!

The key for this book is not to make you a travel expert, but to give you the tools to step into travel yourself and to discover what works well for you. While reading this book, you may choose to start from Chapter One and work your way all the way to the end. Or you may opt instead to skip around, based on where you are in planning your next trip. Figure out what technique would be best and enjoy the journey!

My first trip out of the country led me to Juarez, Mexico, where I found a renewed interest in a language that had only been mildly interesting to my young brain. I decided to study more Spanish in college, and even pursued language school trips in the summers after college. When I eventually backpacked in Europe for the first time, I fell in love with the unknown, determined to travel more regularly. I knew I wanted to go back. Austrian beauty. Italian architecture. Norwegian history. Irish legends. I realized that these people attempted to live slower lives.

In these pages, I have included a couple trips with friends because they were new experiences at the time and still give good insight into planning a smooth trip, regardless of the number of people. I considered methods of traveling more and even took some short-term trips in my mid-twenties. Then in the spring of my sixth year teaching, I thought: *I don't want to be ninety and still say, "I wish I would have gone to China."* I decided to spend four months on the other side of the world.

LONDON, ENGLAND

Chapter 1: Prepare

Now that you are ready to research ways to create your perfect trip, this notebook will help prompt you to design your own itinerary, made exactly for you! My first out-of-the-country trip to Mexico started because I overheard a group of college students discussing a trip that they were taking. At the time, I was a senior in high school, but still curious enough to ask for more information from a leader. This person helped prepare the layout of the trip, evaluate how much each person in the group would spend, and create a list for the group on what to expect while in the country. Most of this was new to me and I scoured the details, a little overwhelmed.

A couple months later when I was on the plane, I felt a little sick, but it wasn't the flying. I was very used to plane travel, as this had been the most common form of transportation when I was kid. When I landed in Juarez, Mexico, it appeared like I was in a desert. Our little group of strangers drove to our encampment for the week, each not yet familiar with the other. I was struck by the dry environment, setting of the houses, graffiti, and the trash. This culture shock did not last long, however, because our group was scheduled that afternoon to do an introduction activity with kids from our program. It was a short introduction, with songs and a couple games, but we got to know the kids that we would be working with for the entire week. There was a lot of laughter among us that night and a lot of exhaustion. At this point in my maturity, I was a quiet kid, but I loved working with children. I had not yet figured out that I wanted to teach elementary students, but there is no doubt that this later played a factor in my decision.

I will share more about this first out-of-the-country excursion later, but let me put in a caveat. This guidebook is the first step to your next travel trip around the world. You will not receive an email from me on what to expect before you head out on your excursion. Instead, you hold in your hands the literature that could help you plan your own trip. It will be personal for you, even if you follow each of my recommendations. This book includes tips and stories about where I've been and what to look for while you are out in the world. The most important things that I will share with you will be how to respect culture, what to do when you are in sticky situations, and how to jump into the unknown, ignoring the fear. No matter how excited you are to begin this journey with me, traveling to other places is a scary adventure. There are many factors that you hope will snap together like puzzle pieces. This book might be able to help you put some of the pieces together before you leave, making things a little less complicated, but will not solve all problems.

What you have in front of you is not a tell-all of how to best travel the world. But it serves as a guide on options that you have while visiting a new country. I still have a wonderful list of places that I dream about, those map pins on my personal "wanderlist", but I also have many countries that I've actually visited, each teaching me how to learn more about cultures and customs. This will cover some broad knowledge, but should be more than enough to prompt you to build your own adventure.

Timing

China was the first country I selected as wanting to visit when I was younger. I decided to pause teaching at the end of the 2015 school year to travel to and live in China, at least for a season. I scheduled the duration of my trip beginning in August, lasting through mid-November because I wanted to be back for Thanksgiving. When you are selecting a season to travel, choose the time that works best for you. Sometimes you land smack in the middle of tourist season, like June in Europe. Other times you choose a month that works for travel buddies, like Germany in January, two weeks after Christmas. Bonus: This last option has fewer visitors, with lots of gingerbread! I would recommend finding a local; a friend who knows the area or a new friend whom you meet within the country. Even if you do not know someone, ask lots of questions. Find where the local areas are by conversing with people in restaurants or parks. My first friendship experience was a friend of a friend offering to show me and two others around Amsterdam for a day. Granted, I did not go on this trip solo, but used a lot of the same methods to plan out and perfect my techniques for traveling by myself. This friend showed us a couple of her favorite restaurants and gave us the scoop on where to visit, which areas to avoid, and "attractions" that were really tourist traps.

If you have the travel bug like I do, you will always want to travel to new locations every month. Practically, you just can't afford that. However, you can always schedule a potentially large trip six months to a year from leaving, and plan several small trips between them. I am always on the lookout for long-term things, but practically, it is sometimes better to schedule something over Christmas break or a long weekend road trip to another state. There are always options to help with that travel itch, and if you love to explore new places, you can always find ways to stretch yourself, even while considering things logically. I will mention this a little later, but you do not want to blow your money on all the what-ifs. You can plan, but do not put your plan into action by buying all the best things in one fell swoop. Make a list, then figure out which is the most important for that trip. Usually, you can buy a few necessary things when you arrive in the other country, too.

Let me help by sharing with you about my first section hike on the Appalachian Trail, which stretches from Georgia to Maine in the United States. It has been a dream of mine to hike the entire Appalachian Trail. So after talking with several people, I decided to start out on a long "section hike," which means traveling in small sections at a time, covering only what I was able to in the span of a predetermined amount of time. My initial goal was to get as many miles as I could in about six weeks. Because of logistics and getting a new job at the end of July, I had to move cities and set up my classroom. In this case, I ended up shrinking my plan to cover four weeks. However, I learned many valuable lessons through this shorter hiking experience that I will use

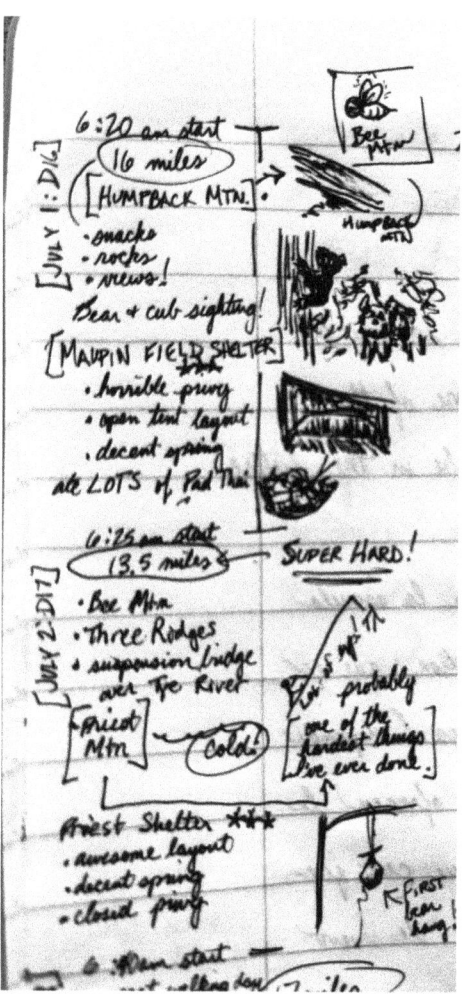

when I am on the A. T. in the future. All this to say, sometimes you can still experience something spending all of your life's savings. You might want to take the big trip, but it could take you several months and some pre-planning in order to get your travel off the ground.

The List

There are several ways to prepare for a trip, and though it took me years to admit it, my mom's way is probably the best. This method is for those of you who want a plan, predictability in the face of the uncertainty of travel. My mom created a list that she would print out every time we prepared for a vacation. It is great for traveling with kids because they can pack themselves. She typed up the list on a Word document with labels for seasons, so the information was the same each time, with items added as we grew.

I take this approach now, but a little more unstructured. In college, I refused to use a list, but I forgot many things. So now, I mainly use Pinterest, which covers the basics, specific to whatever country or time of year I'm visiting. If I look up "Germany in January, packing list", Pinterest will give me list options. I love options. This website includes lots of pictures with each list, including the best methods on packing your suitcase. In my opinion, the lighter you can pack the better. No, you do not need that fifth sweater or the third pair of jeans. You just don't. If this type of packing is not for you, and you would prefer consistency on each trip, you might go with the single list idea.

These are my favorite items to bring, no matter where I go:

- A book - what can I say? I'm a bibliophile and even though I've finally made the switch to a Kindle, I've been in a situation that the power goes out and I must switch to analog.
- Headphones - mine are my around-the-ear kind I use for running, but you might appreciate noise-canceling headphones. I have some for my keyboard and love them!
- Small bottle of hand sanitizer - this goes without saying. Good for everything!
- (Empty) Water bottle - except when in Latin American countries that you can't drink the water. May as well just buy one in the airport.
- Passport holder - mine is as long as a plane ticket because no matter how digital you attempt to be, you're going to receive some paper ones. Plus, you can keep some change and receipts in the zipper pocket and it's easy to find.
- Tennis shoes (or flip-flops) - don't try to be fashionable, especially in the airport. If you're running to catch a flight or standing in a two-hour line, you will want comfy shoes.
- Jacket or sweatshirt - I love hoodies. Even if you end up in Florida or the Amazon, you're going to be glad you have it.
- A converter for the country you will be visiting.
- Ladies: comfy, but cute dress - this has not always been on my list, but there have been a couple previous trips I wished I had one. Just stick it with a pair of flip flops.
- Camera - yes. Just yes. Don't take your most expensive one, but DO have one!
- Charger - this works for the Appalachian Trail and a long flight on a small airplane.

This list does not include the basics. You're going to need clothes, underwear, a toothbrush, sunscreen, and a passport. There is more about packing in the section for United States travel. This is just a cumulative array of items that I use consistently, no matter where I'm visiting. Also, my recommendation: Travel light. Not only will your back thank you when you are booked on the third floor of a hostel in London with no elevator, but you will be less likely to be a target when you walk around with your suitcase. Some people use a theft-proof backpack, but I have never found that necessary. When I am carrying my luggage, I often keep my backpack on one shoulder so most of the items are under my arm. I put my money in several locations and if my phone is on me, it's in my front pocket, not the back. When I ride on a public bus or metro, my bag is either on me, in my lap, or between my feet. The more crowded the area, the more likely I am to keep my backpack in hand. This might not be a foolproof method, but it has worked for me the last fifteen years. If I have my passport and other valuables with me, it is inside a small, preferably zipped, pocket that does not lay along the outside edge of my daypack.

In my opinion, the best method to keep your pack down in size is to lay everything out on your bed. Find the best way to layer in your suitcase, starting with the largest or bulkiest items. You want to carry some of your bulky items to save weight, like the sweatshirt or coat, but I admit, I never want to wear my hiking boots or jeans in the airport. These items, if you are not wearing them, can go in the bottom of the pack. Sometimes, if you get a hiking pack of 50 or 60 liters, there will be a compartment in the bottom for shoes. Nothing valuable should go in this section of the pack. You must have in the back of your mind that you could lose some or most of these items. Do not be too attached to any of your items because you never know what could happen in transit from the airport to the final destination. If possible, consider carrying your pack on the plane. You will then need to double check the airlines for prohibited items and liquid sizes. Light travelers might opt to purchase extraneous items in-country. Others might want to put their entire pack in the cargo hold.

Every person travels differently and the more you do this, the more you will hone your personal "necessary items" list. Speaking of necessary, if you are trying to minimize to the twenty-pound range, step on the scale and weigh yourself. Yes, I know this can be painful, but do it anyway. The travel will be worth it! Then hold your pack and weigh again. Subtract your body weight from the second number and you know how much your pack weighs. Another option is to get a portable travel scale and hang your suitcase from here. Now if the weight in your bag is too much, you might mentally be able to gauge what needs to come out of your pack. Otherwise, you will need to lay out everything again and evaluate. *I like these three shirts* — not five — *and these two pairs of pants*. Not four. If you use materials other than cotton, they will not smell as readily and you will be able to rewear them multiple times. Examples of these are merino wool, bamboo or hemp. You can also find polyester and quick-dry materials, which I prefer over down insulation. If down feathers in a sleeping bag or jacket get wet, for example, it is nearly impossible to dry them quickly.

When preparing for a new venture it is automatic to attempt to convince yourself, "I need to get this shirt!" or "This item would be perfect for my trip!" Sometimes you can. But do not spend your entire budget before you leave. If this is your first solo venture, do not go out and buy a whole new wardrobe. Use what you have. Just keep it minimal. It is better to buy one souvenir shirt later than to have three extras that you never touched on your trip but still lugged around with you. Yes, pack a few snacks. While it is fun to choose from the endless supply of food at the airport, it is more budget friendly to wait until you are in-country. I will explain more on what to expect with budgeting in a following section.

Group Travel

If you are meeting a group — see Chapter Two, "Travel" on the different ways to travel with groups

— after you have signed up to be a part of the program, check your emails often. This will be the primary way your group leaders will communicate. Read all instructions carefully, as these contain specific information for your trip. The first email will most likely be a confirmation and might contain attachments that you need to complete before a certain deadline. It is best to fill these out sooner than later, to have fewer issues to worry about as the trip approaches. You can focus on the fun of packing!

If you have any questions about the trip, check to see if there is a Facebook group or a specific email address to contact. The packing list will most likely include a list of things to observe as you prepare to enter a country. Pay special attention to this, as you are stepping into someone else's country and want to be respectful. If they ask you to wear long pants, cover your head, or travel in pairs, it is not the time to show your independent streak. You signed up to go with this group for a reason and can either back out or do what they say and take notes for what you would change next time.

When choosing group travel, be sure to research well and look at reviews. Make sure they are a reputable organization and are not just going to take your money and run. Also, check that what they offer is something you are able to comply with or willing to learn. For example, when I signed up for a Vacation Race in New Zealand, I was still teaching elementary and middle school and was extremely busy in the months leading up to my vacation. As a result, I chose not to train to run five miles a day. Instead, I ran only two to three miles each day, less than half the recommended training plan for trail runs. Several areas of Texas are flat and I did put in any effort to train on stairs. When I arrived at our first destination, I reminded myself that I was not going to run the entire race each day. In fact, there was one beautiful day by the west coast that I decided to walk the entire trail, other than the downhill portions. I took great pictures and still finished in plenty of time. There is a phrase in hiking that works well for these moments, too. Hike Your Own Hike. HYOH. These travel adventures are to learn more about yourself and the levels to which you are willing to push yourself. Do not compare your journey to others. Instead, be inspired to develop your own plan!

Budgeting

A lot of people ask how I can afford to travel as often as I do. They also nod their head in recognition when I tell them I used to be a teacher. "Oh, yeah. You get summers off." But I also traveled while working an office job full time, taking precautions to plan several months in advance. This allowed my bosses sufficient notice and also gave me something to look forward to. If taking a week off is not available to you, take advantage of long weekends and holidays. Try to travel during off-season months, as there will be fewer people traveling at the same time and flights will potentially be cheaper.

When it comes to saving money for travel, here's the second most common thing people tell me: "You can do all this because you are single.." Well, that is partially true. For anyone reading this, if you are single, too, let me give you some encouragement. You can still travel even if you are living on one salary. You just need to find a way to save money in small increments. When I want to save for trips, I keep an informal note of how I spend money in my personal life. Remember, this is me. You will develop your own system of saving money. Whatever you choose, you will need to document your spending habits in some way, showing everything you buy within a couple of weeks. I am not here to give you a guide on budgeting, but you want to travel, right? You will be able to tell where the majority of your money goes by writing it down. Then you can find ways to limit portions of your money, allocating it instead for travel. There are some areas you will not be able to change, like rent or utilities, but there are other habits, such as eating out, subscriptions, extra snacks, and gas expenses, where you can cut out spending. Maybe you can't nix it completely, but each area of your life is worth evaluating if you want to make a change to incorporate more travel into your life.

For example, one of my biggest spending problems within the last couple years was buying books. It was too easy for me to go onto Amazon or walk into a used bookstore and find good deals. Even though I rarely spent ten dollars on a single book, I would get several in a week. For the 2024 year, January through December, I was determined to cut out buying any new books for a year. I still have over two hundred books on my To-Be-Read shelf, but sticking to my plan has helped me get one step closer to saving for my next trip. The other area I limited partially was eating out at local restaurants or ordering delivery. I still tend to spend more than my fair share at coffee shops because that is where I do a lot of creative thinking, reading, writing, and drawing. But instead of spending twenty-five dollars each time, I aimed towards spending half that. I ordered cold brews over frappuccinos and smaller pastries over full meals. I also calculated that I did not need to pick up food on the weekend when I had groceries at my house. When you look at your own life habits, attempt to find one or two areas that come to mind as you read this section. What is *something* you could either cut down on or eliminate completely to put more money in your travel account?

It is best to budget the cost of each meal for travel, potentially rounding up based on where you are going, and also to set aside spending money for souvenirs. If you are traveling to a more remote area, there will be plenty of outdoor markets and local souvenirs, but you will need to have some cash handy in the local currency, as they will not always have credit card machines. I occasionally use my souvenirs as Christmas or birthday gifts, which makes the gift-shopping experience more unique. I have found it is better to have pictures or journal entries from a trip, or one single souvenir that shows a personal experience. When the recipient knows that the bag you got was hand woven from a tribe you visited, or that you watched as chocolate was made at the factory, you have a story to match to your personalized gift. If you are crafty, you can create a scrapbook or bullet journal. My favorite way to write is through using a simple composition notebook, but you might prefer a travel-specific notebook or one digitized. Audio recordings are more lightweight and practical, but in the end, I find this method frustrating because I later have to write it down again if I am ever to review it.

Budget Specifics

- *Flights*: $2,000-3,000
  - Plane travel can be cheaper if you catch flights six months to one year out.
- *Hotels/Hotels*: $60-$100/night
  - Hostels are cheaper, but you also don't need a super fancy hotel. You will be out exploring!
- *Transportation*: $200/week
  - Budget here depends on the amount of travel from place to place. It can be less, especially if you walk or get a day-pass for a bus or train.

- *Food*: $50/day
  - This doesn't include if you decide to have a fancy dinner. Factor in fun money and souvenirs, too.
- *Tours/Excursions* $400
  - Covers 2-3 tours or extra excursions. Again, it depends on the country and whether you want to create your own walking tours for free.

At each location, you will find your own things to do. Make it your own as you begin planning your travel. The aim of giving you somewhere to start is that you actually *will do it*. Don't let the unknown frighten you. If you are determined and creative, you can figure out a way to earn and save money and see many beautiful locations.

Handling Money

There are several ways to prepare for the money exchange part of your trip. You can exchange currency at an in-country bank or ATM, which might be preferred if you are staying in one area for a more lengthy amount of time. You don't want to have one thousand dollars on your person if you can help it. Banks are very organized and work with you even if you don't speak the language. If you do choose to exchange in-country, be sure to have your passport handy, though not in an obvious location. You can also exchange money at your home bank several days before you leave. This will take one to two days. I more often exchange currency at the airport for short-term trips, but that is the most expensive method of all of these options, however convenient.

When you are withdrawing money for a purchase, do not pull out an entire wad of bills. These can fall everywhere, causing you to take your eyes off the rest of your personal items and not pay attention to the people around you. If you are in a large, crowded area, you are most likely to draw thieves or pickpockets. My personal preference is to have my currency individually folded and, when possible, arranged in order from the largest to smallest bill. I learned this lesson out of necessity and now I can actually reach in without looking and know that I am pulling out one sol rather than fifty soles when I am buying a bracelet from a Peruvian vendor. When you pay for a taxi, know what you are going to pull out beforehand and put away your money and passport as quickly as possible.

You will learn where the best location is for your money and I would recommend filing it in several places. Whenever possible, do not leave your money in your suitcase even if your hotel room is locked; it is likely to get stolen. Look for a safe or an area where your money will be well hidden. When you have bills on your person, follow the same procedures. Put them in various locations so that if you lose one part, you will still have money.

Schedule

Once you have your flight, hotels, and general idea of what you want to do while you are on your trip, write it all down in a detailed schedule. I can already hear you protest: "I am traveling solo for a reason! I want to be off the grid!" Of course you do. Otherwise, you would not have picked up this book. But give the list to someone. You can choose family members, friends, and neighbors, and if you feel comfortable, use an AirTag in your bag or Find my Friends and allow the other person to have login information to see where you are traveling. It is best practice NOT to post on social media that you will be gone on such and such a date. The smarter way to spread your excitement is to keep it vague, or better yet, use word of mouth. There are too many creepers who can hack into your social media account and find the perfect excuse to ransack your house. Rather, it is better to have a big photo dump at the end, to use as a journal through pictures. This is one of those pieces of advice that some of you might blow off, but I just think there are greater risks worth taking.

Do not give up because the preparation is frustrating. Creating a list of your plans will not be something that you look forward to with great excitement. But it is good to have a basic plan. Don't let others talk you out of something that you want to do. There will be people who look at your travel list and state that it is impossible for you to finish it alone. Take their advice with a grain of salt. Listen to what others share with you and decide what you can change if a planned excursion has the potential of danger. Another way to state this, if naysayers present an issue of safety, you can look into alternatives, or travel with one of those go-single, play-together groups that you can search online.

There are always options for scheduling the type of trip that you want. Be sure to find something that is not going to harm you in the process. The right trip will stretch you and lead you to have fun, but also to come back home and share it with your friends. You want to enjoy your trip and anticipate the next. Preparation time gives you a chance to slow down because you don't know what is coming next. You cannot always predict what will happen while you travel. Prepare to be surprised. Accidents do happen, but you can avoid many of these by having a small plan in place and not just walk into something without any consideration. Do not plan something halfway without checking sources because it "just sounds fun". Preaching to the choir here! It is so much easier to just do, not plan, but before you head out, take a couple hours to decide what your route is tentatively going to look like. This will help you to avoid pitfalls.

Determine what resources you have and where you might be able to find more. If you are traveling to a country that is in the middle of nowhere, what is your intention for communication? Will you be able to get a ride in town or will you be going for weeks at a time with little communication? Tell someone. If you are hiking in an area you have never been, see if you can contact your local outdoor store for the best preparations. Do not buy out the whole store, but choose the top three or four things that you do not already own. Figure out where you are going to get your food supply once you make it in country and what items you will not be able to purchase there that you could bring in your packed bag. It is best when you are traveling to think about safety a little bit more than you are inclined to, since you will be working solo. Then you can focus more on the preferential things such as clothes and save the hidden trails as spur of the moment choices.

I am the type of person who determines my routes by reading something, deciding, "That sounds fun!" and then doing everything in my power to make sure that it happens. When you are alone, you can absolutely make snap decisions like this! You do not have to consult with other people. But because you are by yourself, you are your only backup. So in order to do all the things that you want to do, you need to be prepared with at least a basic strategy.

Passport

You will need to go to your government-sponsored website (.gov) for obtaining or renewing a passport. The official website walks you through each step, but here I will explain a summary of the U.S. one so that you have everything in a single place. You will first have to check passport requirements. Your parents might have applied for you to get a passport twenty years ago and you haven't used it since. In this case, you will start over like it is a new passport. I will cover new passport steps here, but the process will be similar for passport renewals.

The first couple steps on the government website cover the basics of your identity, citizenship, driver's license ID, and any special circumstances that might play a factor in obtaining a passport. You will need to send in a small photo that you can easily get by inquiring at CVS, Walgreens, or any pharmacy. There are other options, but I've used CVS for the last couple of passport renewals, which is what I recommend because it is quick and easy. The organization will print out two 2x2" color photos, with some additional requirements. These will change over the years, but at the moment you need to remove a hat, glasses, and maintain a straight face. The background in the photo will need to be plain, either white or off-white with minimal shadows for a clear picture.

Once you have filled out the required paperwork from the website and printed it, you will submit a physical copy of the information to an acceptable post office or government facility. For this you will need to check the website. The passport needs to be applied for six months in advance, ideally, as it will take a couple months to be sent to you. There can be issues with the passport and you do not want to get stuck the week before your excursion with no passport. Another option when you apply is to expedite your paperwork, which will cost more. When you send off your information, they will offer a tracking number, but do not expect your passport in less than a month. That is most likely the shortest time frame that you will receive it. I have not included the cost of the passport in the budget because some travelers already hold an active passport. The information given in this guidebook is primarily for the purpose of using it at the beginning of each trip, particularly if you are new to traveling outside of the country or like to review before your journey.

While you are preparing your passport to be your best travel buddy, be sure to take a look at what kind of travel insurance you have. Sometimes this is covered by your personal insurance, and sometimes you can cover this per trip when you schedule flights (Chapter Two). But since you will be traveling by yourself, it is important that you do not get stuck in another country with no way to pay for a medical bill, in the unlikely event that this occurs. It is far better to pay a little bit at the front of your trip than to have someone bail you out in another country.

Food

Some of my favorite snacks to carry are:

❖ Cocoa dipped almonds — less likely to melt when exposed to heat

❖ Via or another good instant coffee; I found one in Peru that was delicious

❖ Beef jerky with cheese

❖ Trail mix packets

❖ Baby bells — I used these for several days on the A. T. unrefrigerated, and they were still good

Be sure to learn from the locals. Watch people when you enter a grocery store and read signs for what is on sale. What are the areas that seem to be most popular? Maybe you need to try the seaweed chips or the tam tams. If you are at a language school or close to a market, ask your tutors or vendors in the market what their favorite selections are and how they put them together in a meal. Sometimes they will just want you to buy so they will say anything, but these people do this for their livelihood and are very good at their jobs. They know the plants, vegetables, and fruits, and they will be able to tell you what their favorite snacks are.

Always listen to your body when you are trying new foods. Sometimes you will eat something that you are not used to and you will get sick. Find the best way to take care of this, whether it be to visit a pharmacy for the most appropriate medicine or hydration and rest until you can begin your normal activities again. If you get sick, attempt to eat foods that are lower in fats, grease, and spices until your stomach feels normal. If severe symptoms continue, find a way to get yourself to a hospital. It is not the time to be prideful or embarrassed because you want to fully enjoy your trip, and you cannot do this if you are looking for the bathroom every five minutes.

If you are staying in one area for several days, try to get some of your food and snacks from a grocery store. In the long run, it will be cheaper and you will become more familiar with what foods are substantial in the country where you are staying. You should definitely eat at some restaurants. It's part of the experience, but do not eliminate your entire budget on food. Eat smart and try new things to enjoy local favorites and to expand your palette!

That is the main purpose of this book. Use it to explore. It might not contain everything that you need, but it will give you a good place to start. You will be able to get all the basics out of the way and then think practically for the trip that you are signing up to follow next. The world is a great adventure and I hope that you will surpass what I am sharing with you in this book! You will find your own adventures and document them in your own travel blog or podcast. This text is merely a catalyst that will get you started on your journey. In your hands you will find the inspiration you need to motivate yourself to get out there. Make new memories and meet new friends! Discover new things about yourself that you never knew and learn from new mistakes so that you can make better ones!

In conclusion:

- Consider your schedule and plan ahead for travel.
- You can be organized, but don't go overboard.
- Make sure your passport is up to date.
- Learn to travel by yourself, but then be ready to lead others on a journey!
- Spend wisely by thinking things through.
- Enjoy new food from the culture!

Chapter 2: Travel

The world is open to you! One of these days I am going to throw a dart at a map and travel to wherever it lands. There are programs that will do all the work for you, allowing you to have a surprise destination without needing to do the legwork. The itinerary that I explain here in this little notebook is a little more complicated, but it allows you to create a custom trip, designed to travel exactly where you've always dreamed, and save money in the long run. It can be as scheduled or as free as you want! Each of the sections here addresses a particular step in the travel journey, allowing you to design a custom trip. The great thing about traveling solo is that you have the ability to change your mind and don't have to consult a travel mate! At the moment it might seem daunting, but by the end of the next hundred pages or so, you will have a solid idea of how to travel and avoid common pitfalls. You might not be an expert —that comes only with experience—but you will be wiser and more prepared to travel to whatever corner of the world you choose!

Now that you have the basics of what to look for before setting out, this section details the practicalities of getting there. First I will explain the different types of trips you might take. This does not include work exchanges, as I have not done one of those in another country yet. I include how to work with groups who have scheduled itineraries, how to participate in a language school and learn about the culture within, how to find personalized trips, working in mission trip formats with church or medical groups, and even hiking experiences that will really test your wilderness skills.

Additionally I would like to analyze options you have if traveling with children, whether you are a single parent or are traveling for a birthday celebration or the like. There is not a one-size-fits-all when it comes to travel, so I also list blogs that I have found for traveling with disabilities, including resources in the References where you can find more information beyond this guidebook.

Towards the end of the section, I have noted what you need to look for with flights and how to create an experience that is as smooth as possible. Getting to the country is as important as what you will do when you get there. Sometimes that is the biggest step because you might have spent years up to this point dreaming that you *might* do this or could *possibly* do that. Here I am to tell you to GO! Get out there now and take the step towards adventure. I will not promise that it will always be amazingly awesome, but I can promise that it will change you in ways that you cannot imagine. Traveling brings emotions to the surface that you don't realize are there and helps you to build confidence in your abilities. It will teach you about appreciating differences in people, trusting others, and noticing similarities, even halfway across the world. As I am putting this gift into your hands, I do not (yet!) know your story. I do not know even what kind of trip you are planning, but I would love to be that nudge that says, "You can do it!" All you need is to get out there first. The rest will fall into place. It might not be lovely, but it can be wonderful.

Types of Trips

Something you have to decide when narrowing down the trips is to establish your most important goal. As you will be able to tell by reading this book, my favorite part of trips are seeing new places and experiencing how culture and language interact in the development of a country. There are various motivations that push people to travel. Some trips include introductions to different types of food and even cooking classes, so you get to taste your way through a country. This offers insights into how people live, but does not always match a country's everyday life. Other travelers prefer bus trips because there is not as much walking or self-planning involved. These jaunts usually include a very knowledgeable guide, who takes each group through the history of the area. They point out significant places and share memorable stories as they explain about architecture and landmarks. Some people look for trips where relaxation is the key and options for tuning out the world are the only relevant things.

These types of trips include beaches, spas, and plenty of pampering – a perfect getaway for someone who puts work first or has a family constantly vying for attention. Another category of adventures that I advocate are those with lots of adventure. I like to stay busy, so I look for trips that engage me either mentally or physically. I enjoy climbing mountains and exploring back trails. These are just as interesting to me as chatting with people in another language. Each of the trips that you consider are significant in their own way, and I am not going to walk you through all of them. I would like to highlight the importance of first knowing why you want to travel on a certain trip, other than "I need to get out of the house." If you set a goal near the beginning of your trip, this will help guide your decisions throughout the following days.

I will list here several different types of travel, each of which can be approached as a way to travel alone. For the majority of this book, I will focus on traveling while only relying on yourself and your own wits. Each section can be tweaked based on your season in life and ability to travel.

To start, let me share a few favorites and hurdles from my own adventures.

New Zealand: *traveling alone, meeting people or a group.*

The details on this kind of trip are very organized and everything is scheduled down to the minute. This type of planning is valuable for those who like structure, but it is also beneficial if you do not want to spend time planning out every element of the trip. You follow along with the group. This can be especially fun because these types of trips tend to center around common interests. The difficulty is that while these schedules have some limited down time, you need to follow the outline of the itinerary for the most benefit of the trip. If you are not interested in continuing with a plan set by others, keep seeking out alternate options, as this might not work for you at this stage of your life. Your time is your own – except when it's not. This will include those moments when you are getting on flights, traveling with friends, or accompanying a group. You will need to have times when you are willing to listen to others for what comes next in your trip. These events are the most important to getting to where you need to go and maintaining seamlessness when moving from place to place.

I first found out about an international running trip from a different itinerary, in which we were given the chance to run every day and sightsee through a company called Vacation Races. On my latest trip, I raced over to New Zealand for Thanksgiving break. The plane travel was planned by me, but everything else was scheduled to the hilt by our travel company. We had a welcome dinner at the beginning of our trip and those of us who were traveling solo either met

our roommates for the trip or paid an extra up-charge
to room alone for the ten days. I chose to have a
roommate. Each morning we would have breakfast at
the hotel, load our gear on the charter bus, and run
off into the jungle, a park, or around a lake. The
distance was a five- to ten- kilometer trail run, easy to
moderate. Then we would drive a couple of hours
and stop for scenic, locally-vetted places. The primary
locations were not visited often by tourists, so it really
felt like we were getting to explore the country. Our
bus drivers and guides for the week were native to
the region and kept us informed with local legends,
stories about the area, and favorite music suggestions.
These trips were very fast-paced, yet still gave us time
in the evenings. Most of the time we packed our "free
time" with group gatherings or spelunking since we
might never get the chance again. My favorite
memories from each of these trips were finding ways
to push my limits physically, stepping out of my
comfort zone through a cold ice plunge (five minutes
is my max so far!), and getting to know other
adventure-seekers whom I would not have otherwise
known.

Appalachian Trail: *traveling alone, more a part of nature,*
sharing shelter space with others.

I have included a detailed section about hiking the
Appalachian Trail in Chapter Five, "United States
Exploration," which you can flip to as needed. On a
hike like this, you are responsible for setting your

own pace and carrying all your food, water, and supplies in your hiking pack. It is best to start with at least a general outline of how you are going to travel and at what points you plan to stop. You can fit in several rest days as needed, and allow these days to become "bubble days" that can be moved around if you get exhausted or injured and need moments to yourself. You will travel alone most of the time for this type of excursion, working at your own pace, which can be peaceful. When you camp in the evenings, you have the option to hole yourself up in your tent or to listen to other campers' adventures from that day. Many parts of the Trail are isolated, so if you run into trouble, it is best to be prepared to handle it on your own.

I first stumbled upon the Appalachian Trail when I was around eleven years old and our family of five took a short day hike. The A. T. is more than 2,190 miles of a foot trail that covers the east side of the United States' Appalachian Mountain range. I'm sure I might have explored it earlier with my family, but that was my earliest memory of the "real" hiking experience with a backpack, tent, and food bags. It was the first of many trail walks, since my grandparents lived in Virginia. A couple of years ago, I spent part of my summer hiking the A.T. in the span of several weeks, called section hiking. My dad hiked with me for the first few weeks; a life-saver for me! I honestly don't think I had ever even put up my own tent. Needless to say, by the time my dad had his tent up and all his gear inside on that first night, I was still holding a flap to my tent with the rest of the parts on the ground at my feet. Only later did I realize that I had the top part of the tent flipped inside out! After Dad showed me how to set up that first time, it was simple enough to construct, but that night I realized the trip would be a giant learning experience. It was tough at times on the Trail, and I overpacked that first week, close to a forty-pound pack. I learned to spot things I enjoyed on the Trail and have daily tasks to complete. I'll chat about this a little later in Chapter Five. Throughout the month of hiking, I learned to balance both parts: to have fun and to push myself as a hiker. In the long run, the section hiking reminded me how much I love the great outdoors and it helped me to practice the discipline of slowing down. I am already planning to go back to that area and hike the entire trail!

Language School: *short or long-term, closer to culture.*

When you enter a language school, you are expected to follow the rules outlined by the school, but other than attending classes, you are pretty much on your own. There are some opportunities to have meals with other students and days where you have the option to shop for your own food in local markets. Your budget is the biggest variable to watch for on a trip like this because you are more likely to spend without thinking. This practice can add up quickly.

The advantage of language school is that you are surrounded by people with varying skills in your target language. This gives plenty of opportunities to challenge yourself and to occasions to help others.

When you prepare for language school, it is similar to preparing for a solo trip, only the lessons themselves are already planned. Depending on the group that you choose and the country that you visit, you will have options for car pick up, host families, intensive language study, and weekend excursions. My first language school was Guatemala, which I found by typing in "language school in a Spanish-speaking country" to Google. I chose to join the smaller groups because they appeared to have more of a chance to use the language. The longer I stayed in Antigua, the capital of Guatemala, the more I realized that studying a language was more than just learning the vocabulary. I needed to experience the culture, too. During my second week, I discovered how to get to the square and looked longingly at all the books in Spanish, dreaming that one day that I would be able to read the literature in Spanish. I bought one book and a small pocket phrasebook. That was the best purchase I have ever made! It did have a dictionary section in the front, and even more importantly, included commonly used phrases that I would pull out on a daily basis chatting with friends, buying something in the market, or exploring the rest of the town. When I left my first language school, I was by no means fluent, but it gave me confidence in my speaking abilities, taught me how to step into the unknown, and led me to make friends outside of my comfort zone. Later, I would visit Spain and China for language schools and, in the near future, I also hope to spend longer periods of time in France and Turkey.

Group Trips: *discovering things together.*

These excursions are scheduled very similarly to the above New Zealand trip, only you usually find out about these through social media or word of mouth. Initial communication will be sent through emails and sometimes Zoom meetings, depending on the location of everybody in the group. Sometimes you will get the chance to plan your own trip with other friends and family. The beginning elements of trip planning can be found in Chapter One, "Prepare." One advantage of working with a group the entire trip is that you can always bounce ideas off each other. You have the camaraderie of sharing experiences with someone else and building bonding moments. However, when you spend a lot of time with someone, you will see them at their worst and they will see you at your worst. Trips like these can be revealing and exciting, but they can also open you up to be more vulnerable. It is important to listen as much as you share. What an exciting way to learn more about who you are and where you are going next!

My first big trip to entirely plan from the first step to last was backpacking in Europe. Two teacher friends and I were sitting at our favorite coffee shop one October and we decided to plan a trip for the following summer, after we got out of school. Over the next several weeks, we chose places that we were interested in seeing and then narrowed that down to seven different countries. It was a lot, but at the time, we decided to hit several of the "touristy" places so that we would have an idea of what we wanted to go back to later and see. Once we narrowed down our route, we decided where we would start and how we would get from one city to the next. Of course, beginning with our trip in London, England, we *had* to use the Chunnel, the tunnel that goes underneath the English channel, to arrive in Paris, France. One of my friends found other tickets that we could purchase that covered a couple weeks of travel train total, which we could use to get on and off specified trains as needed. This is called a Eurail pass, and I highly recommend it to anyone traveling throughout Europe, especially if you plan to hop from city to city or travel to several European countries. More on this in Chapter Four, "In-country Transportation". We booked hostels for some of the major cities and found a couple tours in Amsterdam, Italy, and Ireland in areas that we most wanted to explore. There were hiccups like strikes and getting lost, but we learned more about each other's goals and what we wanted to do the next time we traveled. Each of us has traveled to many other places since, but we still look back on this event as one of those moments that helped propel us into the world.

Mission Trips: *planned outing, full schedule.*

Mission trips are often planned as group trips, but can also include involvement from other groups who do not usually work together. Sometimes personality conflicts among people can ensue if the trip is not organized from the start, so I recommend trips with meetups during the trip to address any potential issues. There are many people on mission trips, working both with staff from the United States and the country you are visiting. This causes the team to grow together quickly, to build emotional ties and to find common links that otherwise could be missed. Sometimes when people are working together in a busy environment, they might push their personal conflicts aside to address only the missions work. I have experience with both, and recommend that the team take at least thirty minutes to sit and chat with each other as a group debrief each evening. It doesn't even have to include an agenda, but taking a moment for this break gives the group a chance to decompress, laugh, tell stories, and relax. This is much needed in such a high-pressured, rapidly-moving environment.

When I was seventeen years old, I snatched up the opportunity to travel with a mission group to Juarez, Mexico. As I mentioned previously, it was my first trip out of the country and our group worked with different kids every day, playing games and doing crafts. Near the end of the week-long trip, we visited an orphanage. The pastor who had helped us translate all week came with us as our guide. He was explaining what we would see when we walked in and best protocols for interacting with the kids. I thought, *I want to do that someday. I want to be able to reach between two cultures and help them understand each other.* Before this outing I had very little interest in the Spanish I had studied for years, but this encounter gave me authentic motivation. I obtained an education degree with a Spanish minor and the summer after my first year of teaching, I visited another Spanish-speaking country in Guatemala. This was only the beginning of my travel bug!

Travel with Children

There are always options, with a little creativity, to do what you want, though sometimes you might want to share your adventures with little ones! If you are traveling with kids, I recommend starting with Tsh Oxenreider's book, *At Home in the World.* The References at the end of the book includes a section of my favorite travel books (so far!). Oxenreider's book explains that traveling with kids is similar to solitary travel, just at a slower pace, and includes visits to a few more kid-friendly areas. Children can learn about new cultures and gain an appreciation for change when they travel to other countries. They might not become history buffs, but what might happen if they develop an appreciation for science, anthropology, or languages? Every child is different and will respond to travel in their own way. When your family travels together, you will learn about each other and support each other through the journey.

If you are a single parent traveling with one or more children, you might need to go through some extra hoops. I will point you in the direction to get started, but you will need to complete several steps, especially if traveling internationally. In some separation or divorce cases, the parent traveling with the child must have proper identification and often a notarized letter of consent from the other parent to cross international borders. There are many procedures to protect the child above all else. Every country is different in how they approach a single person with a child, so follow the link in References to check the country you will be visiting. These and additional legal information about traveling with children can be found at https://www.usa.gov/travel-documents-children .

Two of my favorite sites for travel with little ones are listed below:

- Big Brave Nomad - https://www.bigbravenomad.com/

There is one article by the Carlsons that I found

particularly helpful titled, "Seven Best Tips for Traveling with Kids as a Solo Parent" that shares what to keep your eye out for when traveling solo with kids. Everything is laid out from flights and packing to using technology and conducting activities with kids. Each section highlights a particular issue and contains how this family has successfully persevered while traveling.

- Single Mom, Strong Traveler - https://singlemomstrongtraveler.wordpress.com/

Written by a mother of five children, this blog follows a mom who explores the world and tests out brands from both little-known and well-known companies. She helps her kids explore the world one adventure at a time. There are stories about each of their wanderings as she relates how she gets to know her kids while they grow together.

There are also articles and tips if you search for "single parent travel with kids," "Traveling as a single parent," or if you look up "Activities for kids' travel" on Pinterest.

Alternate Travel Options

It can be difficult to motivate yourself to travel if there is something else that you have to manage. Just because you have a disability or are nervous about how you will appear to other people does not mean that you must abandon your dreams. You might just need to approach things from a different angle. I've included below information to help you take the next step in travel, even if at first it seems impossible.

I will be completely honest here. I do not have a disability, so this has not been a consideration for me while traveling. However, after watching my friends and others with disabilities travel successfully, I definitely would like to include tips here. Throughout this research, I have attempted to find a mixture of personal blogs and practical articles, highlighting the adventures of each trip. It is my hope that you find someone whom you can connect with; someone who will prompt you to explore on your own, even when it feels intimidating. While the following is by no means a comprehensive list, I anticipate that you can use this section as a springboard for your own travel research. Don't let the hurdles trip you up! With a little bit of help, you might just discover your next great adventure!

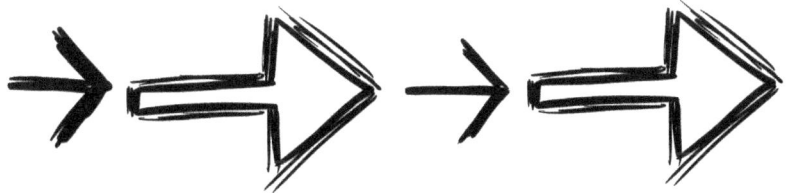

"30 Best Vacations for Wheelchair Access." World on Wheels, 2 Feb. 2024, worldonwheelsblog.com/blog/best-vacations-for-wheelchair-access/.

This blogger shares her experiences traveling around

the world in a wheelchair while also offering tips on navigating the airport, insurance, and activities while on vacation.

"7 Accessible Travel Tips for the Deaf & Hard of Hearing." Rescu Saves Lives, 25 Sept. 2023, www.rescusaveslives.com/blog/7-accessible-travel-tips-for-the-deaf-hard-of-hearing/.
An article that explains processes for personal safety, airport routes, and flight questions.

"ASL Deaf Tours in Spain, France, Italy, Portugal, & Europe." ASL Deaf Tours In Spain, France, Italy, Portugal, & Europe, 2019, deafeurope.com/.
This webpage shares blogs and articles on various countries around the world. It hosts announcements on the best way to travel and how to find the applications that you need to enjoy your journey.

Bear, Chelsea. "How to Plan a Solo Trip with Accessibility in Mind." Trip Advisor, 2 Oct. 2023, www.tripadvisor.com/Articles-lxnxdomT3qQA-Accessible_solo_trip.html.
Chelsea Bear explains how to overcome hurdles of traveling with a disability. She also gives tips on staying organized to get the most out of solo travel.

Blind Girl Adventures, 2024, www.blindgirladventures.com/.
This blog, written by Sassy Wyatt, tells of her

adventures as a traveler from the UK who is blind while still experiencing the far corners of the world.

Blog, Hostelworld. "Backpacking with a Disability! (South America Edition)." Hostelworld Travel Blog, 26 Oct. 2018, www.hostelworld.com/blog/travelling-with-a-disabi lity/.
George doesn't let anything stop him! In this article about traveling to South America with cerebral palsy, George shares several of his favorite places to visit and tips for sightseeing.

"Catch These Words." Catch These Words , 2024, catchthesewords.com/.
This webpage, written by Conner Scott-Gardner, includes a blog and tips on traveling while blind. He shares personal stories and what to anticipate when setting off on a solo adventure.

"Group Holidays for Blind & Sighted Travellers: Share the Adventure!" Group Holidays for Blind & Sighted Travellers | Share the Adventure!, 2024, www.traveleyes-international.com/.
These planned trips include multi-sensory opportunities for people who are blind and people who are sighted. Solo travelers are paired together to help each other experience the world.

Marson, Laura. "How to Emotionally Prepare for

Solo Travel." A Dynamic Life, 18 Mar. 2024, www.adynamiclife.co.za/how-to-emotionally-prepare-for-solo-travel/.

Laura Marson explains in this article about how to find the small joys in solo travel, adjust expectations, and to prevent strong emotions from having the final say.

"Solo Travel Blues: Dealing with Anxiety, Burnout and Loneliness on the Road." Northtrotter, 22 Feb. 2023, northtrotter.com/2023/02/22/solo-travel-blues-dealing-with-anxiety-burnout-and-loneliness-on-the-road/.

Northtrotter explains her success in traveling solo for many years. At the same time, she gives practical techniques on what to do if experiencing strong emotions. She lays out steps to follow, distractions to refocus, and activities to try as you explore the world.

Nesbitt, Tracey. "How to Conquer First-Day Solo Travel Anxiety." Solo Traveler, 29 Jan. 2024, solotravelerworld.com/conquer-first-day-solo-travel-anxiety/.

Traveling can be scary. Tracey Nesbitt addresses this by sharing practical advice when traveling solo. She takes an experience that might be overwhelming and gives basic solutions to breathe, distract yourself, take a break, and enjoy the moment.

"Solo Travel for Introverts: The Best Tips for

Traveling." Salkantay Trekking, 30 Mar. 2023, www.salkantaytrekking.com/blog/solo-travel-introv erts-best-tips-traveling/.

How to plan for a trip when emotions run high. This article lays out what to expect and how to handle solo travel when things get overwhelming.

Sygrove, Carly. "Flying with Hearing Loss: Best Airlines and Airport Travel Accommodations for People with Hearing Aids and Implants." HearingTracker, 28 July 2023, www.hearingtracker.com/resources/flying-with-hear ing-loss-airline-accommodations-and-travel-tips.

Detailed steps on traveling in the airport for those who have cochlear implants or hearing aids.

"Three Best Destinations for Deaf Vacations." ETIAS News & Information For Visitors Coming To Europe, etias.com/articles/deaf-vacation. Accessed 2024.

An article for tips on what to look for when seeking out vacations with accessibility. It includes explanations on what travelers who are deaf can expect in Spain, Sweden, and Switzerland.

"Travelling Solo with a Disability." Just One Passport, 25 Feb. 2024, justonepassport.com/2022/06/27/travelling-solo-wit h-a-disability/.

This webpage is written by a senior woman who loves

to travel. She shares a blog of her experiences and gives
practical advice.

"Wheelchair Accessible Travel Destinations."
Wheelchair Travel, 6 May 2023,
wheelchairtravel.org/destinations/.
Itemized list of destinations around the world, ideal for
wheelchair accessibility. Categories are sorted by the
United States and Canada, Africa and the Middle East,
Asia, Europe, and South America.

"Wheelchair Travel Map Destinations and
Guides." Inclusive Inc, 2024,
inclusiveinc.org/pages/travel?gad_source=1&gclid=
CjwKCAjwyJqzBhBaEiwAWDRJVDKmqvwtp3M6E
MZcwKnxXqRK1_9vLFPRnl5U9-KsJ3A8VLcuZXMjY
RoCsaYQAvD_BwE.
Links and travel tips for mobility in a wheelchair.
Kristin also has a blog attached to this site.

Flights
Buying plane tickets is tricky because this section
of travel is so unpredictable. I will one day book with
a company that does all this for you and sends you on

a surprise vacation, but until then, I have to plan how to get to my destination. The Kayak app is my favorite to use for this because it keeps everything in one place. This was a friend's recommendation once and I have not looked back! You put in the dates and time that you are interested in, and it gives availability for flights. This app will also help you book hotels, though I do not often use that feature. I like to put these in my favorites list by tapping the heart to see if the flight changes over the course of a week. Finding flights is not an exact science. You can choose a multi-trip option to include various stops in your plan. For instance, I've used this before when visiting a friend and, later in the week, my grandparents. It gives the flexibility of doing "all the things" while maintaining the convenience of being all in one app. More in the References section of this book.

On my latest trip to Peru, I was aiming to meet my group at a certain time and later to break off alone and fly to Cusco without spending twenty-seven hundred dollars. I split the trip and ended up spending twelve hours in the airport at two different layovers. Make sure you are okay if you book like this, but I was *happy* with the alternative over only having an hour to swap planes in an international terminal or spending half a paycheck on flights. You will decide for each trip what works best for you in this regard.

Sometimes a flight gets delayed, and you have the option to put your name on the standby list for an earlier flight by going to the gate's customer service counter. You can also add your name to standby when you are at the main ticket counter, but usually you will have completed customs/check-in already, so the gate area will be easiest. Standby is a little different, and sometimes you do not get booked a seat number for your ticket. This means that you will have to wait until you are called, conditional as to whether or not there are extra seats available. If you are lucky, you will grab standby on a fairly empty flight and be issued a genuine ticket.

As a note, be sure to include some sort of travel insurance when you fly internationally, whether this be through your regular insurance or the trip that you are scheduling. You always have multiple options for this, but double check that the insurance that you purchase 1) is legitimate. This can be evaluated by looking at several types and following recommendations of others who have been in your shoes. And, 2) covers everything that you will be doing (or plan to do) on your trip. Sometimes it is essential to find a short flight from one town to another, usually on an airline that only flies in-country. This must be done through the airline's website, but can usually be found through Kayak or Expedia as well (see References), if you want to keep all your flights together.

Leave more than enough time for flights. If you live near a small airport, you might only need an hour for check-in, especially if you are carrying everything with you. It is better to wait around for an hour than to crash through the gates ten minutes before your flight takes off. No matter the precautions, you might have days when everything seems to go wrong. Your second alarm didn't go off. You didn't drink your coffee. The check engine light goes off in your car and you have to wake up your friend to drive you to the airport because there are no car pick ups at four in the morning. You wait in a line where there is only one person who is working the counter because of short staffing issues. The person ahead of you complains about everything. Someone loses something in their suitcase and opens the entire bag onto the airport floor. Breathe. You will find an alternative.

On one trip I was waiting for a flight from Lima back to the States and the flight was delayed until the next day. I requested to refund my flight and reschedule on a different airline instead of waiting until the next day for the follow-up flight. I waited in the airport for more than five hours, but aimed to catch my flight to the States the next morning. The gate boarding area was a tiny, one-room section of the airport, so I grabbed a couple of snacks and my book. I would stand up every once in a while to stretch. By the end of the day, I caught the flight!

No matter what, there is only so much control you can have when traveling. There are many factors to consider and you will need to evaluate the best courses of action. As much as you can, do not get upset to the point of yelling at staff or crew. They are doing the very best job they can in the position they are in, usually answering to another person. If you remain as patient as possible, at least outwardly, you will have more benefits than if you lose your cool. This is not easy. You can still be insistent, but not obnoxious. Include "excuse me" and "please" while you are talking with someone. They have a lot to handle every given day and because of this, it makes their job difficult. Try to include an appreciation towards them, even when things don't go the way you expect, even when it seems like there is no good answer. This was a trick that my dad, a retired airline pilot, told me. I spent many hours in airports throughout my life and saw both sides of this coin. There is always a solution. Sometimes it just takes work. Most of the time when you encounter a problem that frustrates you, watch the people around you to see what they are doing. They might help provide an answer.

In conclusion:

- There is more than one way to learn about a country.
- You do not have to be by yourself, even if you plan alone.
- Find a way to get there, even if it looks unconventional to others.
- Go for it! Seize the day!
- Get on your first flight and start the newest chapter in your life.

Chapter 3: Housing

This is the part where it gets weird, especially if you have never stayed in a hostel before. The "family style" setup always reminds me of bunk beds at camp. When you enter a room, most likely you will be staying with eight to twelve other people. You can claim your bed by unrolling your sleeping bag and putting a book or hat or something not valuable on top. It is common to leave your stuff in a locker somewhere in the room or under the bed, which is often a shared space with your fellow bunkmate. Always zip up your bag. This is not just to prevent stealing. It is to protect from any creepy crawlies in the night. Also, do the same with your shoes. If you cannot put them in a bag or the corner of your suitcase, lay them upside down on the bottom corner of your mattress. It is better to sleep with your items than to find a tarantula inside them the next morning. Also, speaking of unwelcome visitors, you might encounter wildlife in your housing area, whether that be a cabin, hotel, or hostel. Yes, there might be mice or cockroach infestations. Ants could possibly be crawling on you in the morning because you left an opened Snickers bar on the dresser next to you the night before. It has happened!

When you arrive in the country, it is best to find a taxi or a service to the hostel. Hostels do not consistently offer this, but you can check with them beforehand on what transportation they suggest. Regulations are always changing. Be sure you get all your luggage. During my first day in China, I had to figure out how to communicate that my luggage did not arrive at baggage claim. This gentleman did not speak English and I did not speak much Chinese. So I got out my phrasebook and began trying to explain that my luggage was lost. Did I mention this was 10:30 at night? He looked up a couple things on his computer and talked to some people on the crew to help find my bag. It was an orange bag, only a little bigger than a backpack, but the previous flight had been so small that they had required me to check it. Not only did this gentleman help me find my bag, but he also called a taxi. Whenever you find yourself in a similar situation, or someone calls a taxi, you should ask how much it costs and be sure that you know if tips are expected or allowed. In many places in Europe, for instance, tipping is already figured into any total cost.

Reminder: Do not leave all your money in the same place. Have several different locations that you will stash things. Always keep your most valuable items within easy reach, but out of sight in a zipped pocket and not in any back or outside pockets.

Hostels

I love staying in hostels, but be careful: You have to check reviews. It is so easy now to inspect a hostel because of available apps created just for this purpose! People who travel to hostels can give references, updates, and recommendations on what is nearby. There have been a couple of times where I mistakenly booked at a hostel with a similar name to the one I wanted, but in reality it was farther than my sightseeing plans, the train, or the airport. Always double-check the address!

Hostels do not necessarily need to be booked more than a couple days in advance. If you are in a big city or an area where you will spend a lot of time, you will want to plan accommodation locations before your trip. When you get there and you have a reservation, you usually pay right then. Some hostels will only take cash. If you are like me and do not carry cash, you might need to use an ATM. These have an expensive exchange rate, but are still a feasible option in most cities. You can always go to another hostel, depending on time of year. If you've paid a deposit, you might lose it, but sometimes convenience wins out. A couple of situations like these will give you a sense of what kind of traveler you are! Attempt to stay calm, even if check-in is hectic. At times, you will get there early and cannot go to your room for a couple hours, so some hostels give you the option to put your bags in lockers or a secure location as you travel around the city. The same can be requested after check-out at most hostels, so it's worth at least asking.

I used to set a travel alarm clock. Yes, the kind that has the little button on top, hands that light up in bright green, and that has a really annoying beep so that you don't sleep in. For the most part, there is electricity available in hostels. Currently, I use my phone as my alarm and make sure it is charged the night before. Don't forget your converter! If you are using an Apple charger, these will be fine, but the connections are sometimes oddly shaped and you will need the converter anyway, depending on the country. Other times, it is fine to use the USB port, such as on buses or planes. You can always check with a fellow passenger or the hostel's front desk before you fry all of your electronics.

A day pack is perfect for most explorations unless you are moving often from place to place. In this case, you will need to carry your whole pack through streets, up stairs, and on subways. Again, I recommend that you keep your initial pack to 20-25 pounds (around 11L). Once you have settled in, take a look around. Walk around the area, go back to the lobby, ask about any recommendations on places to eat (definitely) and places to see (probably). Ask if there are any spots that locals enjoy hanging out at or if there is a must-see activity in the area. These questions might surprise hosts a little because they are so used to offering the same suggestions to tourists, but you could find some "off the beaten path" elements for your trip. This is how I learned about several side quests. Ideally, after I find one recommended location, it leads to another place, or a chance to just sit and relax, like my friends and I did in Paris for a couple hours while we waited for the lights to appear on the Eiffel Tower. We grabbed crepes and sandwiches off a street truck and sat down for an impromptu picnic after visiting the Louvre. If you are ever in Paris, it is an ideal place to see art from history! I was not even following my art passion then, but it was amazing, and I wish I could have spent more than one day in that museum.

When you have completed your first or second day, you will want to get a better layout of the city. Walking is usually best for this venture. It allows you the freedom to get lost or to find little nooks you would not otherwise know existed. If you have a particular destination in mind, like a certain restaurant or a sightseeing location such as Big Ben, then you might need to find transportation. I will include more details about this in the next chapter. Ask at your hostel or a nearby person before you start. That will save you some frustrations on your first day in the city.

Also during your introduction to the city, it is

imperative that you stop and breathe. This is something that, even though you are tired, frustrated, or experiencing a little culture shock, will help you immensely. Stop and take in the sights. Maybe you experience a little of the culture by spending a couple hours on a terrace, the patio of a restaurant. You could decide to stop on a bridge to observe the water, people, and boats. This is something best done without the camera, at least for your first day. Take a

☑ **REMEMBER:**

Do not leave anything out at night. It is easiest to sleep in socks or have socks right next to you so that you can walk to the bathroom in the middle of the night. Everyone will come in at different times. There will be varying levels of noise. In order not to disturb neighbors as much, prepare what you will be wearing the next morning and place it near the top of your bag.
If you know you are coming in late at night, have your pajamas and toiletries accessible so that you can easily grab them.
It is great to have a little flashlight to search for belonging when it is dark, or you can use your phone.

second to step out from behind the lens and let yourself sink into the culture. There will be many more opportunities to play tourist, but for now, attempt to live in the moment. You can appreciate what you have accomplished simply by being there, to let yourself be proud of where you have come. You made it.

When you return to your hostel, do not leave anything out at night. It is easiest to sleep in socks or have socks right next to you so that you can walk to the bathroom in the middle of the night. Everyone will come into the common room at different times. There will be varying levels of noise. In order not to disturb neighbors as much, attempt to prepare what you will be wearing for the next morning and place it near the top of your bag. If you know you are coming in late at night, have your pajamas and toiletries accessible so that you can easily grab them. It is great to have a little flashlight to search for belongings when it is dark, or you can use your phone. Just try not to shine it in a fellow sleeper's eyes.

The first night might be rough because you are getting used to a new bed, time change, noises, and sleeping with total strangers. The question arises, *Can I trust them?* Whether you can or not, you are going to have to. Most people in the hostels are between 20-35 years old, leaning more towards the younger end, but you will find everyone of all different backgrounds, each with a different story. Almost everyone is there in the midst of travel. The great thing about hostels is that you get to set the tone for how friendly you are. When you need your space, you can ignore other guests and they will leave you alone. If you want to chat, you will easily find someone to talk with. Sadly for us morning people, this camaraderie will not be possible at 6:00 in the morning, unless you find someone at breakfast who has already guzzled their coffee.

Hotels and Airbnb

I will explain more about hotels in Chapter Five, but I'd like to describe an encounter when I was in Cusco, Peru. The owner of the Hotel Ureta, Victor, was very friendly and chatted with me about my travels and my writing. I found out on my last day in Cusco that he was still struggling to get out from under debt since Covid four years before. The hotel itself is situated just outside the busy parts of the city, only about fifteen minutes from the airport and within walking distance from the main Plaza de Armas. Victor struggles with health problems, but loves the Cusco town and the people who come to explore. It is interesting to find hotels run by locals that still have a personal touch. Everything was clean and tea was available at all times during the day. Spending a couple days before and after my hike helped me get acclimated to the altitude in the area and gave me a chance to explore the town. If you stay in hotels over hostels or an AirBnB, you have a chance to put yourself closer to places where you can learn from the area. Don't get stuck in your room. Rather, get out and explore, as you would with a hostel. Talk to waiters and store owners about their recommendations for the area. Even if, like in Cusco, you are compelled to speak another language, carry a phrasebook with you to minimize nervousness. The difference in what you can learn and experience is so much greater if you attempt to overcome a language barrier..

More information about renting an Airbnb is clearly outlined in the app, found under the References section. It is an easy-to-follow format that allows you to choose your dates or location and to evaluate the quality of room that you would like. Airbnb options are designed to give you a little more privacy, while still enjoying the community. If you are traveling for style, you can rent your own cabin, or you can go as simple as a room connected to someone's house. The locations vary and you are able to evaluate the quality of each place by reviews placed from previous tenants. The owners are good about staying in contact with you from the very beginning, even if they run several residences. You will also receive a survey afterwards so that you can credit your thoughts on your stay.

Language Schools

Sometimes travel involves a language school. This

is whenever you visit a country for the purpose of learning the language of that culture. There are also opportunities to travel as a teacher of English, which would be a similar school setup, but since I have never officially been a language teacher in another country, I will leave that to the experts. If you want to stay in one area for an extended period of time or are visiting a country for the first time, language school is something you might consider. Some travelers are also perpetual learners. I've participated in different versions of language schools, and how you plan depends on what kind of experience you desire to undertake. Your options for housing are varied, ranging from staying with a host family in your own room, in an apartment with a roommate from the school, or bunking in a private room. Each of these have advantages and disadvantages.

Host Family

With a host family, you must follow the guidelines of the house, given to you at the beginning of your stay or posted in a prominent location. Sometimes you are asked to keep a curfew, and at other times you are given a key. You are required to eat certain meals with the family, which gives a phenomenal chance to practice the language. Sometimes there will be other students from the language school, but often families cannot afford to host more than one or two visitors. This setup is the best advantage money-wise because the meals are grouped in one price included with your stay and you often have weekly chances to tweak the type of package you would like.

Roommate

If you choose to live with a roommate, they often, but not always, speak English. In one rooming situation in China, roommates were assigned to each student, paired with English Language Learners across the street from my language school. My roommate was just beginning to learn English so our conversations were conducted in Mandarin. That is one way to dive deep after a month of studying! Some disadvantages of having a roommate are the different schedules or the possibility that you might not be as compatible as you would like. You have someone to go to lunch with on the weekends, but often, even if they speak the same language as you, they are not familiar with the area either, and you must find ways to explore.

Private Room

The third kind of stay is one where you have an individual room. This is good because you have more privacy, but it can get lonely. You have more of a chance to explore. You must be deliberate in getting to know people in your language school because otherwise you will be exploring a city on your own.

Every language school is different, but typically you have an option to study with your teacher and classmates for either half a day or a full day. I have worked with both and it depends on what you want to get out of your trip. If you spend half a day, the second half can be used for sightseeing or other excursions near your establishment. This could get expensive if you're spending all your time and money at the market or hiring official guides. If you work a full day on language study, you do get the evenings to explore some of the nearby restaurants, stores, and bars, but sometimes you might be tired enough just to go straight to your lodging and watch a movie or read. Both study options are great for increasing your knowledge of the language. You get opportunities to dive into vocabulary by the book and with native speakers. After participating a couple summers of intensive language study, I will more often choose the half day study because I have learned how to best study vocabulary and have more flexibility to hang out with fellow classmates and tutors. You will have options on select weekends for excursions around the area. These are set up to learn more about the everyday culture of the country and to get to know your classmates better. These could either be offered from the school or outlined in a brochure from a collaborating vendor.

If you find interesting things in the area that you want to explore, go for it! Don't wait for someone to invite you to a new restaurant, beach, or nearby park. Invite them! If there are people you know a little who are already planning something, politely ask if you can tag along. Be cautious about the situations you put yourself into, but know that most of the time at language schools, you will find a group of people with similar interests. If you like to go out every night, practice your language skills, explore the city, jump into adventurous activities—all of these will be available! You just need to make a little effort to find them.

Camping

My favorite form of camping is by setting up a tent and camping out in the wilderness. Not fully under the stars, of course, though I have laid a blanket down under the stars for a few hours. Bugs would love you if you decided to lay out in the elements overnight. Always do your best to find some sort of shelter. I go into more detail about the ins and outs of tent camping on the Appalachian Trail in Chapter Five, titled, "United States Exploration".

Besides tent camping, there is RV camping, which I've only done a couple times. This is very convenient to travel to the next road tripping destination on the map, but you must learn to be resourceful and practice working in tight spaces. If you are mainly hiking or exploring during the day, cramped quarters should not be too much trouble. The setup can be a little time consuming and you must find a good location. The food preparation in an RV is easier because you have a little stove and even a refrigerator, so you do not have to be quite as frugal as when you are camping on the Trail.

Glamping is something I have only done once in Peru, while hiking the Inca Trail. Each person in the group had porters to carry the main bags, who went ahead of us to our daily campsite, set up our tent, and served our meals each evening. It was a unique experience to hike with newfound friends, but I prefer the simplicity of carrying my own items with me. Other than the strenuous task of hiking, I have considered a few more relaxing tree-glamping places that will soon make it to the top of my wanderlist!

In conclusion:

- Find a place to stay that you feel safe and that suits your purposes.
- Learning a language can be as interactive and as intensive as you want.
- Don't forget to put yourself into the culture, not just learn about it!

Chapter 4
IN-COUNTRY
TRANSPORTATION

Chapter 4: In-Country Transportation

Arriving at a new town can be daunting, even under the best of circumstances. You will most likely suffer from jet lag and either be wired from the large coffee you grabbed before your last flight or dead tired, ready to collapse for a couple hours! Whatever your next decision is, do not spend the next three days in your hotel room just because you do not know the city. Some of you will be ready to attack your plan the second your feet touch the tarmac! Others will hesitate in the lobby of your hostel because you are unsure of where to go. No matter where you find yourself at this junction, do not allow any location on your agenda to stop you. Everything is new at this point! Even if you have been to a certain country before, you might have not been to this exact area. The people are different and the smells are unusual. So embrace it! Look around and take it all in.

The first day my friends and I were in Venice, we wanted to find a dinner place and there was a restaurant that my parents had recommended called Rossopomodoro, an authentic Italian restaurant. It was my dad's favorite place to get pizza and he knows his pizza! The city is a maze of passageways and very tall buildings, not to mention the channels of water everywhere. It was absolutely breathtaking, but we were starving, so we wanted to find a place to eat and had no idea which square the restaurant was located near. No matter what road we chose, we wound up wandering in circles and in several instances, the walls between the buildings grew significantly smaller–no joke! When thirty minutes later we ended up turning into back our apartment complex, we argued about what to do next. We did not have Wi-Fi, but my friend figured out that we could open the map on our phone and follow the blue "you are here" dot to navigate our way through the city. So for the rest of our time in Venice, we opened up our map to follow the little blue dot to get our bearings through the city. Happy conclusion: We did find the restaurant, unfortunately closed until the next day, but we ate on a little patio area which sold delicious lasagnas. I was no longer complaining!

You might not necessarily use our method of the little blue dot, but you will have to navigate areas that are unfamiliar and figure out a way that works for that situation. It is helpful to ask people who live nearby, but it is also possible to allow yourself to get lost. Turn down a side street just because you can. Give yourself the time to take the wrong road until you recognize something. Sometimes you will need to be on a deadline, but when you have the chance and the area is new, it is best to become familiar with the layout of the land. The quicker you allow yourself to do this, the more the unknown place will transform into a new home away from home.

Walking

When you arrive on the first day, it's best to not have anything planned because you never know what will happen with flights, buses, or other connections. Afterwards, you can walk around the area to familiarize yourself with the best routes and locations to note for later, and quite possibly find some unexpected surprises. There could be a strip of restaurants or the head of a hiking trail for you to explore the next morning. While you watch the bustle of people, you will get a feel for what kinds of transportation you'd like to get such as a tuk-tuk, metro, or taxi, and to gain knowledge of where each is located. I have definitely walked the wrong way in Paris for twenty minutes. At night. With a map. If you tend to be directionally challenged like me, it is essential to get your bearings by looking at landmarks or street names. The more familiar you are with a place, the less likely you are to waste time. On that note: If you do waste time, remind yourself that this is a vacation and that you are getting a chance to see more of the local scenes!

General Transportation

Decide how you are going to get to your hotel, hostel, or Airbnb. Most likely it will not be on a main street. You can take a bus if it is in the middle of the city. Then you have to decide if you are going to go back to the train station the next day and how. Sometimes numbers are at the place you are staying, but a lot of times for remote places, it's better to book beforehand in an app or online. Finding a bus station or taxi is the easiest way to go, but not if you do not know where you are going. Try to have your locations written down in one place. Then, even if you don't speak the language, you can hand the driver your destination address to check that they know where to go. When taxis or a car service needs to be hailed, be prepared to pay. They do not often negotiate and occasionally charge more than you think necessary. It is more common to decide on a price before getting into the taxi. In China I got a couple rides from a new friend on a motorbike. It was crazy, but he knew what he was doing and most of the time while in-country, I tried to walk as much as possible, or save change or get a day pass for bus transportation.

Another thing I was introduced to in Paris was the subway system. Depending on where you are in Europe, it is called the metro, subway, or Underground. When I went to Paris with my friends, it was confusing because we all knew very little French and were not accustomed to how the train system worked. Another method you can implement is to count the number of stops between each switch, double check that the stop is listed as the one you are wanting to reach, and make sure the train is going in the right direction. Most of the time, a line is named after the last stop on the rail. If you are traveling some distance, it is more than likely that you will have to switch lines before reaching your final destination. Never fear! There is usually more than one way to get to where you want to go. Take your time at first and after a couple days, you will be a pro!

This will all depend on the country you visit. Latin American countries most often have tuk-tuks, which are three-wheeled taxis. You will need physical currency for these trips. These drivers are pretty reliable if you let them know where you are going and ask for a price at the beginning. If they will not give it to you or demand more, you can walk away. Sometimes you can debate a price for a ride and other times you cannot. But at least you will not get stuck at your destination short of money or arguing with a stranger in the middle of the street. The same can be said of individual transportation in China, but you usually pay before you leave, and you cannot haggle in most areas.

My favorite way to travel is by train, but the metro works similarly. It's a little less pre-planning than the train, but usually you can only book limited days at a time. You can also find bundles of public transportation based hourly or by days under "metro ticket" that includes buses, metros, and in certain areas, water taxis. These can get costly if you don't calculate how long you are going to be in one location, but worth it if you are conducting your own walking tour of the city. Evaluate which type of transportation would be best for your schedule. Another fun option for Europe is the bike, which charges by the hour, or electric scooter tours. These are great ways to get farther than by foot, but also to stay close to the community. These are available in various U.S. cities as well.

Eurail

The first time I rode a train was in Europe, and we calculated that the Eurail paid for itself within about five uses. It sounds expensive, but it is something you should consider, especially if you are traveling to different cities within one country or are expecting to explore more places around Europe. I have included information about the app and website in the References section. Once you have the ticket, you are sent an email and can download the app on your phone. This is what you will use each day when you get on the train. There are different bundles that you can purchase, with each giving a special package deal based on the price you are willing to pay or the length of your stay in the

country. The rate that I chose two out of the three times during travel in Europe was one that could be extended for three weeks, but also gave me the option to skip several days in a row. This was useful when I wanted to stay in one town for several days, like with Germany, but was also invaluable when I transferred from one city to the next, such as moving from Venice to Florence, then to Rome.

With a Eurail pass, you will need to update each day you travel by filling in the designated mark for every time you use your e-pass. The ticket then refreshes for the next twenty-four hours. If you do not do this, you might find yourself on a train with low internet access trying to pull up a ticket. Your second option will be to pay for the one-way ticket, though sometimes you get lucky and are able to refresh the pass.

Metro

The first way to get to the metro is to find the sign that has a U inside a red circle for several European countries or a prominent directional sign that says metro. You will need to walk into the open area and find the computers on the side of the wall. They have tickets that you can order, based on whether you want a day ticket or a ticket just for a couple of hours. This all depends on what you are planning to do while you are in the city. If you are just wanting to see the sights, a day pass might be all you need. Select the options for English or whatever language you feel most comfortable speaking. You will choose the area that best fits the parts of the city that you want to see, pay the given price, and your ticket will come out of the bottom slot, along with change, if applicable. Sometimes you can find an option to purchase more than one day at a time, but the method is the same. When transferring from country to country, your Eurail pass works the best, but you will want to either take public transportation or the metro for your in-city travel. Be sure to keep an eye out for coupons or deals because you can find packages if you evaluate the best options rather than jump into the first ticket options available.

Once you have your ticket, swipe or click your card for the entry area to the platform and the bar will rotate. Check the wall map for which direction you need to head, and times for when the next metro will be available. There are clocks above each platform with countdown timers updated with each passing vehicle. You will need to determine how each transport system works because it is slightly different for every country. In general, you will find the platform that will connect you to another line or railway. You have a limited amount of time to board, so be sure to have your bag with you when the metro pulls into the station. Inside the metro, you will usually find a map or hear an announcement as you approach the next station. Also, be sure to check the platform name on the sign when you pull in, as this will keep you from getting lost. If you do not recognize a certain area, you can always get off the metro and double check the main map on the platform again, which can show you what connections you need to take. Once you approach the correct number of stops, you will exit at your destination and travel through a tunnel. This will lead to sets of stairs that will bring you back up to the street. If you have a map, you can follow that to your next place. If not, you will need to look for signs to where you are attempting to go.

This can be confusing if you come out on the opposite side than you were expecting, but give the system a couple days and you will get very accustomed to this form of travel. It is a wonderful public transportation system to use, especially if you are wanting to explore various parts of the city!

Train

As much as I love flying to new places, the train is by far my favorite! It is comfortable and gives me freedom to walk around. Usually there are giant windows where I can observe the countryside as it whizzes past. Even if it takes a while to get to my next location, it reminds me to slow down. Sometimes I look out the window, and other times, I take the opportunity to pull out my book and read. When I do not constantly check directions, I can settle down a little bit.

The train is often connected to the airport and is a wonderful way to travel among different countries and nearby cities. Sometimes your passport will not be needed because of the border layout of the countries within Europe. Even if you are staying in one area for an extended time, it is a good idea to use the train for day trips around the area, to become more familiar with the surrounding countryside.

When transferring from country to country, your Eurail pass works the best, but you will want to either take public transportation or the metro for your in-city travel.

When you decide on train travel in an area where you need a passport, be sure to book this ticket well in advance. You will need to arrive at the station at least an hour early to check in with passport security and to scan any luggage that you are carrying, similar to catching flights in the airport. There are information desks that can help you if the directions on the ticket are unclear. I have personally misunderstood this process and had to regroup and remind myself that a couple hours of delay was not the end of the world. It was a situation that reminded me that flexibility is key when traveling. Anything can happen, and it is best to either have a backup plan or to evaluate an alternative when something does not go according to plan.

Check the signs on the train doors and the side of the train to be sure that you board in the second class area, unless you pay for first class. There are usually crew members who walk throughout the train to check tickets and passports when necessary, so have your ticket within reach, but put it away somewhere safe afterwards. Sometimes you will sit next to people and will want to switch seats. Depending on the time of day or the city that you are in, there will be other places to sit, but do not count on the guarantee that there will be additional seating areas. If you are just transferring for one stop, you might choose to stay standing in the waiting area, the open space by the doors in between train cars.

Most of the time you do not have to stay seated on a train. Sometimes there are large windows to view the countryside or a vending machine located on either end. There are bathrooms in identified locations of certain cars, so look for the small toilet signs. When the train is within a few minutes of pulling into a station, an announcer will let you know which station you are arriving at. You can gather your items and stand at the head of the cars, going through the front or back door, to wait in the loading area for your train to stop. If you are unsure about your stopping places, ask the people next to you or, similar to the metro, get off and check the map. Trains stop for longer periods than the metro, but this also means you might need to wait longer to board the next one.

Other Forms of Transportation

Bicycle

I've mentioned this a couple times, particularly when I went to Spain, but biking can be a favorite pastime even within the United States. It is a healthy form of transportation and gets you to your destination quickly. Many cities have designated cycling areas for you to move safely through the city, even with traffic. It is difficult to carry things with you while on a bike, but not impossible, so decide if a small backpack or a basket in front might work for you..

Bus

Do your research because buses in London will be different from buses in South America. Buses like those in London are meant for a lot of tourists, and will include stops for attractions around the city. If you grab a bus in Peru, you could be in everything from a large van, fifteen passenger bus, or a tourist contraption. Bus drivers are often very skilled at their job, though at times can make their passengers very nervous. A lot of times traffic signals are more like guidelines and the bigger vehicle has the right of way. In this case, it is better to carry on a conversation with your seatmate in busy traffic than to watch the crazy maneuvering from the window.

Ferry

Ferries are slow and peaceful methods of crossing a river, a channel, or simply bringing you far enough away from the shore to take beautiful pictures. I imagine my trip through Venice, Italy at night and it is breathtaking to see the lights of the city, people on the bridges, and reflections in the water. I've also used a large ferry to cross from the mainland to an island. Personally, out of all these additional forms of transportation (one of these days I'll get to ride a camel and can add that to the next edition!) I think the ferry might be the most magical way to transfer from one place to another.

Moto/Moped

These are very fun to ride and they are easy enough to maneuver. This form of travel is highly useful for people with lower income to use motos over cars, especially in cities with heavy traffic. The moto serves two purposes: 1) It is easier to weave in and out of traffic, even when carrying an extra passenger (or four!). 2) It is more efficient gas mileage and saves the family money. This form of transportation is prized for convenience, especially for working people with medium to large families. Tourists are able in certain cities to get rides on motos, as well as in tuk-tuks, three-wheeled covered vehicles, which are utilized similarly to motos.

Trolley

Often cities that have higher population areas will use trolleys over buses because it is better for the environment. It is equally as convenient as a bus because there are set schedules where you can stop and disembark multiple times on a route.

Not all opportunities are listed here. There are many other ways you can explore the city and get to know the culture around you. My point is this: Don't always feel like you must stick to the "tried and true" method. If something doesn't work out, try something else! If you have a chance to go on an electric scooter tour or take a trail ride on the back of a horse, by all means, make some memories! You are the one shaping your vacation. Design it to be personal!

In conclusion:

- Do not get stuck in your hotel room.
- Make friends with the local transportation system.
- You might have to ignore your nervousness and go explore.
- Avoid some pitfalls of traveling in another country.
- Find different ways to travel so that you can see more on your trip.

Chapter 5: United States Exploration

On a normal day, it is difficult to find time to travel, even if you have the inclination. One of the best ways to start out on travel adventures is to find a location near you, within a couple hours of driving. I have met many people who say that they want to travel, but something always happens to get in the way. "I don't get enough time off at my job." Or maybe, "I can't afford it." For a lot of people, "I am just waiting until the kids get a little bit older." You've made it this far in the book or maybe you skipped over here immediately because there is no way you are even going to consider escaping the state, much less the country! You definitely have a legitimate excuse. Everything revolves around family and you need to make enough money to pay the bills for your apartment. You do have to set aside extra time. When you save up for a trip, you will have to say "no" to certain things. The question is: What are you willing to *do* to start that trip that you've been dreaming about for months?

I am all about day trips. But if you want to push yourself, try camping overnight somewhere, a relatively cheap option that also gets you out of your normal routine. Next thing you know, you'll drive yourself to another town to take a pottery class with a group of artists or make a road trip to Maine just to try the fresh lobster! Whatever adventure you have in your head, there is a way that you can figure out how to do it. You just need to take the first step. Camping is perfect, especially if you have kids, because things are more localized and kids can learn more about interacting with each other and with nature. Information about single parent travel is included in Chapter Two, "Travel." Try going for a hike, with the option of camping under the stars. You can grab this chance on a weekend because no matter where you live in the United states, you are just a couple hours away from a park, camping ground, or hiking area. Don't think erroneously that you must spend a ton of money to do something different. Twenty dollars will allow you to view many places.

As long as you travel, you will need to develop a sense of direction, however you choose to do that. It is never a good thing to constantly get lost and build more frustration as you attempt to enjoy a city. You can get a compass, a battery powered GPS system, observe landmarks, and ask directions. Whatever works for you, continue doing that. Better yet, improve all these techniques because you will constantly learn something new in whichever city you explore. You will develop your own system, but will also hone that system with every new experience and learn to tweak your method based on the circumstance.

In this chapter, I will peruse a couple of different trips throughout the United States, basics about the Appalachian Trail, and how to avoid emergency situations.

Traveling with an Agenda

My purpose for passing through California, Pennsylvania, and Canada were for writing. In Santa Barbara, I was able to attend a workshop of a writer I follow, Allison Fallon, and thoroughly enjoyed her workshop on how to write a memoir. This was ironic since until that point, I had only ever written poetry or journal entries and was knee-deep in the rough draft of my first contemporary novel. This guide will probably be the closest that I ever come to writing a memoir! That Santa Barabara trip could not have been farther from what I needed in my career, yet it was exactly what I needed emotionally. I had just gone through a breakup two months before and thought I would be living in California at the time. It turns out that every attendee of that workshop had traveled at least an hour to get there! None of them lived in Santa Barbara. And no, to my disappointment, there was no Psych paraphernalia, since most of the shooting for the TV show was filmed in Ontario, Canada.

When I visited Philadelphia, I researched ghost stories for a future historical fiction mystery in a touristy town called Bethlehem. I arrived just after

Christmas decorations had been set up, so I experienced the charm and timelessness of historical houses with battery-powered candles and tour guides dressed up as colonial residents. I went there primarily for writing, so I scheduled an Airbnb close to the area I was planning to explore. As much as possible, I prefer walking or taking local transportation as opposed to renting a car. However, the more you travel the city, the more flexible you can be with other options. More details about "Transportation" are in Chapter Four.

You can always meet up with friends for a day, planning your travel along a route where you know people. One wonderful thing about traveling more is meeting people from other places! Then you can drop in for a quick visit as you journey to your destination. When you are traveling by car, always have in mind whether you need to get a hotel or stop by the side of the road for a couple hours, but the more fun option would be to spend a few hours with a long-lost friend or a relative who lives nearby. Take a look at "Travel" in Chapter Two about how to find the best flights and to plan a good route for your trip. The next section in this chapter includes finding transportation from the airport in the U.S. and getting around in the city once you are there.

If you are taking more of an explorer vibe and are not as concerned about a schedule, you can instead search for "Hidden gems in [whatever town]" or "tour like the locals in [city name]". This will lead you to many unusual opportunities which you might not have considered exploring. My favorite way to do this is to use Pinterest because I am an artist and this website has a lot of pictures. It can get dangerous because it will give you similar ideas to your search and lead you down the neverending tunnel of brainstorming. However, if you need motivation, this is a great way to start! One thing will lead to another, I can guarantee it.

Whether you find yourself in a city or small town, always find a place to enjoy your surroundings, preferably with at least a few people. You might be traveling solo, but it doesn't mean you have to be a hermit. In Pennsylvania, I found an amazing walking park and some good sidewalk space. I was running at the time, so it was a good excuse to see the town and take pictures. There was also a local coffee shop that sold food like sandwiches and wraps. These are my favorite types of munchies because they offer more substantial food and I can wander longer without getting hangry (hungry + angry). This particular place was also near a bike gear shop, as biking was huge in the area. Two things I learned from this: 1) Be open to fun opportunities that might not have been on your list, and 2) Find a comfortable spot to do your work. Even if you work alone, it does not mean that you'll always wander alone. I talked to two different people in that coffee shop over the weekend who made a recommendation for an authentic Italian restaurant (amazing cannoli!) and who showed me some favorite sites in the town. These encounters are my favorite parts of traveling because getting to know the culture enriches the experience, drawing you into daily life even more, and it usually costs less than sticking only with tourist traps.

Transportation in the States

This section takes into consideration how to find transportation when you do not drive your own vehicle. A lot of travel within the United States might include road trips, especially with the cost of flights nowadays, but this will help you not be completely lost when you land at the airport.

If you have not booked a car already with the rental company in your destination town, you will follow signs to the car rental area. Sometimes this is not a big deal because there are plenty of extra cars. I have even upgraded one of my trips because the small vehicle I requested had not made it from the other rental company. There are times when you arrive in a city and there is a big celebration going on or a large group arriving that night which did book ahead. The customer service counter can help you with options for those situations. It is as easy as showing your license, looking at the payment information, deciding how you are going to pay, and being prepared to return the vehicle in excellent shape and with gas. If you do not bring it back with gas, you are likely to incur a fee that is far more exorbitant than refilling the tank.

In some areas, your hotel is close enough to opt out of getting your own vehicle and instead take public transportation. When you are looking at bus schedules, confirm with the driver which direction you are going and double check that it matches the intended bus line, as multiple routes can merge at each stop. Again, if you make a decision and decide to switch vehicles, you are always free to change your mind! When I was in one city, I rented a bike for a day because people in that area were very observant of cyclists and it gave me a chance to explore the city even more thoroughly!

Another public transportation backup is to use a car service like Lyft or Uber that can pinpoint where you are. This does take some observation and you will need to carefully monitor your steps. Each driver will have a system where you can pay through the app or with a card, and you can even look at previous ratings. Usually when you call the service, they will communicate where they are through the app and you can verify them through their license plate and identification badge on the front of the car. I have used this method in remote areas and in cities with success, and this will work for you, as long as you are willing to pay for mileage. I personally think this is one of the easiest ways to get from one area to

another, but if you are staying at
a hotel, the host at guest services
will also explain options you
have as you explore the town.

  Some of the best ways to see
places around your area are by
taking a road trip. This also
works well if you are on a tight
budget. While choosing to drive
will rack up gas bills, it is
significantly smaller than plane costs if you are
traveling within ten hours of your desired
destination. The great thing about road trips is that
you do not have to limit what you carry quite as
much and you have the freedom to travel with
animals. If you pack things in your car that you end
up not using, you can just keep it in your vehicle.
Also, road trips now have the convenience of using
GPS (Global Positioning System) whenever you're
driving. I am glad this was developed right around
the time I was learning to drive as a teenager because
maps were the hardest things to get used to. I was so
directionally challenged that my dad even gifted me a
laminated map when I received my driver's license.
Now it is easier for me to find landmarks to help me
get my bearings within the city. This is relevant
whether you're in San Diego or Sao Paulo.

United States Hotels

While you are searching for a place to stay within the United States, you can choose both cheap hotels and Airbnbs, which are fun and interesting to book, based on where you will be located. Do not look for extremely cheap hotels unless they are through a very well-known chain because I have gotten lice from a seemingly clean hole-in-the-wall place. Hotels that are of good quality also might have a gym, a pool, Wi-Fi, and even a continental breakfast that is included with the price of the room, so be sure to ask about amenities like this.

Bed and Breakfasts used to be considered a thing of the past. Now there are places that will let you rent rooms and even full-sized bungalows. The program that I use the most is Airbnb. Most Airbnbs have the basics like a bed, tub, even a small kitchen. I have included app details in the References, and you can pull out your phone to quickly scan other expeditions near where you are staying. They will give you details on the host and the location of the stay, as well as multiple pictures you can skim as you are making your decision to stay. Some star hosts include goodies and extras for you to enjoy throughout your trip. This is a fun choice if you want to experience something a little closer to the culture you're visiting.

There are other times that you would prefer to be alone and rest, with everything at your fingertips and a place to exercise and swim. For that I would choose a hotel. The front desks will have great recommendations on local cuisine and attractions. Be sure to ask about any local events happening during your stay. It's a good opportunity to stumble upon the unexpected and experience something new—sometimes for free or at least very cheap! If you are going to explore the town before traveling to your next location, you can ask the front desk to hold your bags on your last day. It's not always a guarantee, but many hotels will do what they can to accommodate you if you choose late checkout or to lock up your bags. If you do set out with your bags, you can carry your smaller pack with you while shopping or keep everything in a locked storage area for a certain time at a bus or a train station.

On the Appalachian Trail

The A.T. is a good way to condense how you spend money, but there are many factors that you must take into consideration. Hiking all day is a strenuous activity even for those who are in good shape. The Appalachian Trail is a more than 2,190-mile rolling-hill footpath from Georgia to Maine, or visa versa, if you so choose. This is a time where you find out what kind of stubbornness resides within you! You will encounter weather issues, shelter, food balance, and wild creatures. When you are first starting out, you must consider the size of your pack and essential items, food and water-filtering elements, shelter options, and most importantly, the weight that you are willing to carry. You are transporting your livelihood on your back for however long you choose to stay out there. I section-hiked for several weeks in West Virginia and Virginia a couple years ago, and will someday soon hike the entire Appalachian Trail! It has been a huge dream of mine and will continue to spur me to jump into new challenges!

Packing Supplies - A. T. Style

The following list includes what I kept going back to while preparing for the A. T. As stated in Chapter One, "Prepare", you will find some things that work better for you. Try to find the smallest, lightest piece that still gives you enough of the product for a couple weeks. You can always restock in towns, but sometimes you must think creatively. Put a large trash bag inside your pack (I used 60L, but was a little big) to help keep everything dry. This is my packing list that covers what I included, but as you hike more, you will develop your favorites to add to your own list.

Clothes (Warm weather)

- Long-sleeved shirt (x2)
- Short-sleeved shirt (x2)
- Pair of shorts (also use as pajamas)

- Waterproof pants
- Socks (5-10 pairs)
- Underwear (5-10 pairs)
- 2 sports bras
- Other toiletries
- Rain jacket
- Trail or cross-training shoes with rock plates
- Plastic poncho, can be really cheap
- Flip flops/camp shoes
- Bandeau/bandana (I also use mine as towel)
- Hair ties, carry on my wrist

Hiking

- Sleeping bag
- Sleeping mat
- Tent, individual setup
- Footprint for tent
- Hiking poles, MUST
- Pack cover
- Toilet paper roll, without cardboard
- Poop shovel with duct tape wrapped around handle
- Survival bracelet (x2)
- Mosquito bracelet

Necessities

- Passport or driver's license

- 2-Liter Smart Water bottles (x2), empty for the plane
- Sawyer filtration system
- Odoland camping pot and stove, similar to the one I used
- Portable Bunsen Burner (x1-2)
- Spork
- Small container for washing utensils
- Cloth for washing utensils
- Travel soap, nothing fancy
- Headlight, batteries removed
- Bear bag and hanging apparatus
- Aquifer
- Moleskin, MUST
- Antiseptic wipes
- Dry shampoo
- Regular shampoo
- Retainer/Mouth guard
- Razor
- Fingernail clippers, also used as scissors
- Reading glasses
- Hand sanitizer
- Lip gloss, with sunscreen
- Sunscreen, small
- Phone/Wallet
- Cord for electronics
- Portable charger
- Medications

Other

- Sketching pages or journal
- Pens and pencils with eraser
- Kindle, in plastic bag
- Headphones
- Tank top
- Baseball hat (I didn't use)
- Tiny Uno
- Paracord bracelet
- Medium waterproof bags that close, extra

Food

When you first start out on a trip like hiking the A.T., you will enter the store and look around for snacks that are light, yet filling. Weight on these long hikes when you are carrying everything on your back will always seem to increase as you go. The total weight of the food needs to be considered because it quickly adds up to an additional ten pounds in your pack every time you restock. That does not include the water, outlined next, which will weigh four pounds when the bottles are filled. Each morning on the Trail I would boil water, have coffee and maybe oatmeal (Dad preferred this) or trail mix. My go-to snack on the Trail was a bagel with peanut butter and the occasional baby bell cheese. When you are packing, put all food in large, zipped plastic bags because everything is packed out and no trash cans are available on the Trail.

The foods I ate the most:

- Some freeze-dried meals that can actually last for two meals
- Dried veggies
- Trail mix
- Crackers, put in container with lid
- Peanut butter
- Bagels, a few
- Beef jerky
- Oatmeal
- Via, instant coffee packets
- Ginger chews
- Baby bells, top of pack, lasts for several days
- Hydration packets for water, MUST

Water

I mentioned in the A.T. Supplies list that I used two Smart Water bottles, but really, any water bottles would work. I reused these for about a week at a time because I liked how they fit in my pack, they were light, and they each held two liters. It was perfect for a day, and if there was a stream on the Trail, I would fill the bottle again before continuing. This is not enough water if you are walking in desert conditions for days at a time, so if that is the case on your hiking adventure, you might want to consider a camel bladder bag.

My dad found a Sawyer water filtration system that worked wonderfully for us! It took a couple clumsy tries, but I finally learned to stick the bladder bag under a well-flowing stream and squat down to wait for it to fill. I could either put the cap on to carry it back to camp or attach the filtration nozzle to one end of the bladder and the water bottle to the other end. It was easiest to set the bottle on a rock and squeeze the water through the filter, which takes several minutes. But during one very desperate stretch of trail to get to a shelter when I was in Virginia, I stopped by a shady shelter that had horrible, yellow water. It was my only option for several hours if I wanted to hike all the way to the next shelter. I used the filter system and smelled it before trying the filtered water, but it was as clear as glass, with no particles inside! I highly recommend this method.

There are other options, such as one that my friend gave, with a filter that comes attached to the inside of the water bottle and you can immediately drink the water after pouring. Then you could also get the iodine pills that you drop in your water. You have to wait about thirty minutes for this method. Another option we always had was to use our stove-boiled water after it cooled.

Shelter

I am so grateful that my dad was with me on the first night of the Trail. Here I was, a thirty-something-year-old and I had never put up my own tent! I stood there with the instructions out on the ground and the impending storm headed toward the campground. Once I realized that the footprint sheet needed to lay right next to the ground before putting the tent up, I was in business! Then I learned how to line up the poles into each hook of the top of my tent and to hammer stakes into the ground with a nearby rock. After this one simple procedure, I was able to put my tent up alone the rest of the summer! This small, covered area was my escape and my own personal space. As a natural introvert, I realized that I needed that. If you are an introvert, you might find Chapter Two, "Travel" interesting, specifically the section about Alternate Travel Options. When you find a location at or near the shelters, you are not alone. It is important to find time to decompress after such strenuous exercise. While it is fun to chat and hang out with other campers, I prefer having time in the morning or right before bed to write or listen to music.

Another option on the Trail is to carry a hammock, which provides the option to hang out anywhere, regardless of any rocky or steep terrain. However, this works better during hotter seasons because you will need to include an extra layer of padding underneath your sleeping bag to block the wind or inclement weather. You usually cannot keep your pack in your hammock with you, so between the options of hammock or tent, I chose my two-person tent. This was perfect for me because I laid all my items on one end of the tent and very few of my clothing items got dirty, wet, or stolen.

I cannot leave this section without mentioning the bear hang. Apparently this is not as much of a thing the farther north of the A.T. you walk, beginning in southern Virginia. For the first 300 miles (I had started from Harper's Ferry and worked my way south), tall hooks were available at shelters or there was occasionally a bear box. The bear bag must hold everything at night that has a smell so as to keep away unwanted creatures that you *will* find on the Trail. Besides the food, I would also put my deodorant and toothpaste inside. By the time I was on the last week of my hiking excursion, I used my bear bag, found a tree with a branch that was at least twenty feet tall, and threw my rock attached to the rope. It took several tries before I successfully hooked the rock onto the tree, and I still never quite figured out the best way to tie it. I hung several of these afterwards, and even once when it was difficult to find a spot, slept with my bag, sealed everything inside really well, and put it inside my pack. Though I don't officially recommend this for your trip, sometimes you have to do things out of desperation.

Emergencies

It is easy to say you are prepared and that you've covered all your bases, but you must practice steps for unexpected situations, at least once. Make sure that you have walked yourself through how to change a tire on a car. Practice putting a splint on your arm only using one hand. You never know if you'll have to walk five miles to the nearest clinic. Work on a few simple knots in case you need to pull something up or drag an object. Do not walk into situations like week-long hikes without either having a direct line to the outside world or having practiced a few basic first aid procedures. Moleskin padding is my favorite thing ever for cuts and scrapes. You can trim it to the size you need. After washing your wound out with an antiseptic wipe or flushing it with clean water, dry it off and apply antiseptic. You can put the moleskin directly onto the cut, or even better, with a bit of gauze or a bandaid underneath. It will not stick to the scab as it forms. The Moleskin is meant to stay on as long as possible, protecting the scrape from the elements as the cut heals. In one particularly gruesome glass cut, I switched out my Moleskin bandage often until the wound closed. Afterwards, I kept it on the cut to keep it clean.

Always have a basic medical kit with you, even if it's a small one, and be prepared to use other items, such as a sleeve or a bandana, when emergency situations arise. You can receive training in first aid online, which I did one summer in college when I was a lifeguard. More information about first aid courses and basic emergency training can be found through the American Red Cross in the References section.

In conclusion:

- Traveling in the States can be a snap.
- Finding places for work and fun will bring a new perspective.
- Look for areas that are close and convenient for small trips.
- Challenge yourself by living off the grid for a few months.

APPALACHIAN
TRAIL

Chapter 6: Making Friends

Traveling solo might get lonely at times. There are moments where you are riding a train and everyone else is asleep. You can read, watch the scenery go by, or walk between the aisles. Then when you enter a new town, you might find a restaurant and people watch. You can walk in a park and follow a family who has little kids, glad that you do not have to wrangle little ones at the moment. But in all this activity, you can go for an entire day—or longer!—without actually talking to someone. You should look for chances to chat with the receptionist at the hotel, other travelers in the hostel, a barista in a café or someone walking their dog in the park. Yes, there will be moments that you will be glad you travel alone, with just your own voice as company. But the more you are involved with those around you, the more you will create memories. You can converse with people who come to the same coffee shop every morning and discover that a botanical garden is hidden within walking distance from the restaurant. You can find a walking tour that occurs every day to explore the history of the town. Take a bike route to find new pathways to explore. The more you wait for the lesser-known things to emerge, the more excitement you will find in the mundane. It will surprise you to learn that you do not always have to be entertained, yet can enjoy the ordinary. Those are the things that you are going to remember because they touch a part of you that is there to learn more about who you are. There are revelations to be uncovered from travel, *especially* if we are not looking for them! Travel is a chance to try new things, and when we attempt to form new patterns, we open up different tracks in our brain. We build new pathways mentally as well as physically and emotionally throughout our journey. This is not a counseling session, but it can be! More about these brain pathways can be found in Dr. Caroline Leaf's book, *Switch On Your Brain*, which is noted in References.

Local Knowledge

Spain was my first month-long trip, and I did not realize that I had to step out and make an intentional effort to get to know people. I had booked a language school where people entered and left classes about every two weeks. I was staying with a host family, a single lady who had an extra bedroom in her flat. She fed me every day because I had requested it when I signed up with her. A couple weeks into my month-long stay, I found that it was more beneficial to eat out occasionally with friends because I had chances to get to know more people and practice my language skills in various situations. We tried both new and customary dishes, comparing reactions to foods. I'm willing to try anything at least once, but to this day, I still do not like mussels, shrimp, and beets. The seafood in Spain was always fresh because our tiny town was relatively close to the sea. An adult Spanish student that I met even gave me her copy of *Far from the Madding Crowd* (Thomas Hardy), which she had picked up in an airport and planned on leaving in her room. I like that idea, and it's one I would like to implement in the future. I did not get to know these language travelers as much as I would have liked, but it taught me not to get stuck in a routine, to ask questions when needed, and to go with the flow.

That first venture overseas was a pitiful attempt at making friends, but it taught me a lot. I assumed I would get to know people in my small language groups, but they rotated through so quickly that when I got to know someone, they moved back home. When we had evening activities, many were overcrowded or very few people attended. If there was time to chat, it was at the beginning because once the event was done, everyone scattered to their evening activities. Once when I was in Spain I tried bar-hopping with friends because tapas is an extremely popular and normal way of life. It is different when you are all sitting around a table chatting with wine, goat cheese, and cracker spread than the noisy bar where you can barely hear anyone and your friend bumps into you because he's too sloshed to stand. That is not the kind of socialization I prefer. Sometimes new experiences will be worth exploring. Go for it! Do not avoid something just because it makes you uncomfortable. But if something doesn't feel right, don't force it. The time will come for you to take the leap. Listen to your gut and do look out for yourself, especially if you feel uncomfortable..

I determined that hanging out with a couple people or individuals was more my scene. We had funny chats. I found out about their "real" lives outside of language school, and we explored new areas together. I wanted to do things I did not have the chance to try in my everyday life, and this was true with how I made friends, too. Before I began traveling annually, I would let a friendship develop organically and not consistently seek out chances for conversations. I was able to find friends by asking if someone needed help with the coffee press, inviting someone to a noodle restaurant, or going to the football (soccer) game in the square the upcoming evening. Sometimes I would ask, "Hey, is there room for one more?" if there were several people inviting others to a restaurant. Every traveler's experience is going to be different and your approach might be different from mine. This can get a little sticky because you do not want to insert yourself into a group that has already formed a friend group. Then you would just be a fifth wheel. That does you no good. But if you stumble across a diner that serves amazing pizza and is having karaoke one night, why not be the person who invites others? At one point, a small group of us language students created a habit of visiting an authentic Indian food restaurant on Friday evenings as we discussed weekend plans.

The great thing about travel is that nobody knows you. I do my best to be polite to others and respect the culture I'm a part of, but sometimes I put my foot in my mouth. Either way, I have learned that making friends is not about molding yourself into the "ideal" friend. It is about being available in the moment and being vulnerable when needed. Once I inputted myself into a conversation and gave my opinion to students who were not even talking about the topic I thought they were! One girl was scheduled to be roommates with me on an excursion until she decided to switch cabins because she was homesick and wanted to speak her native language. I was part of a conversation in Spanish with a native from Spain

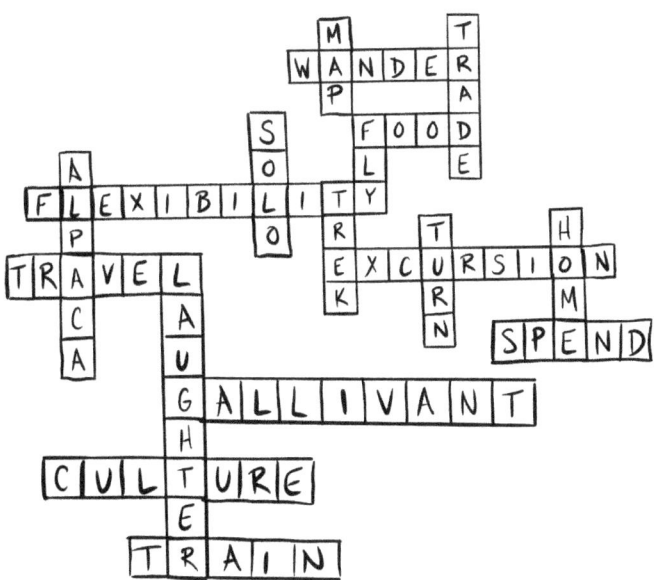

about places I had seen in my travels and he recommended areas for my next visit. A guy on a bicycle tour kept the door open for me on the train. A new friend gave me her travel book before she headed back to the States. A woman opened up to me about the anxiety she was feeling at work and explained how travel was reminding her to smile. A family with two young children was in China learning the language together in order to live there for a year. An artist chatted with me about selling art on the street. One of my tutors stressed the importance of communication first before reading and writing because connections with people are the most important.

Friendships and Fries

When traveling solo, it is easy to have the mindset which states, "I must do it like this and I will do it all myself." But it doesn't have to be that way! Recently when I was working with a medical missions group in another country, I was suffering from something that seemed like an illness. It had continued for several days, but nobody whom I talked to was able to pinpoint what was wrong. I was shivering at the end of the day. Fortunately, I was with a group for two more days before splitting off for my solo excursion. On the fourth day of this weird illness, I was standing in the sun to get warm when one of my friends grabbed me and stated, "Hannah, you're going to get your vitals checked." My blood pressure was good and I didn't have a fever. But my blood sugar level was at 55. The average person should have levels between 80-120. I was immediately sent to a back room with a liquid IV drink, a coke, apple crisps, and chocolate, with orders to lay down for a minimum of thirty-five minutes. While walking there I nearly passed out, and one woman told me that I was slurring my words. It's really frustrating when my brain knows that I should be fine and my body is not cooperating. I bounced back within two hours and have never been so excited to feel "normal," especially when I spent the first part of the trip feeling sore and rundown.

Part of traveling is about sharing adventures and supporting others on their own adventures. This is why I encourage you to find your own style as you travel. Everyone has their own personality and therefore, their own preferences. You will find a method to explore which works for you and it will most likely change by your next venture. However you choose to approach this, you might still elect to travel by yourself, but it doesn't mean that you must endeavor it alone. Stay in contact with family and friends. Two of the best forms of communication are to use WeChat or WhatsApp, depending on which country you will be visiting. I have used WhatsApp the most. This gives you a form of communication to share significant steps in your journey, not necessarily spreading it around on social media. I will emphasize again: It is not wise to tell the world your exact location at every given moment. This opens yourself and even your house to a lot of unnecessary danger.

You must be careful while traveling not to lose compassion for others. Yes, traveling and stepping into other cultures does give you reminders to be thankful, chances to try, and experiences to test out. If you are not conscientious, however, you can lose compassion for your fellow humans. This sounds intense, but hear me out. Traveling has opened my eyes to new sights and customs. It has taught me to laugh at myself when I make mistakes. I reach into messy, unfamiliar situations to see what I can handle, and I am proud of myself. Despite all this, if I'm not intentional, the exploring can become all about me. What I have experienced. Where I have been. And that's *not* why I travel at all. That might have been the true reason you snatched up this book: "I want to go SOMEWHERE!" Travel is a lifestyle, not just one trip. Even if you take one trip a year or every ten years, your experiences on that journey will change you – guaranteed! The key is to maintain a compassionate mindset, rather than a selfish one.

Mindset is something that you must establish and constantly evaluate, even in the middle of your trip. This is important when you share part of your adventure with others. Despite your great adventures, your friends might have a meaningful background story that needs to be shared.

- One woman wins her battle with cancer.
- A man is starting his medical training.
- A girl has aspirations to be a dentist.
- Someone shares a chance to practice English.
- A new friend tears up as she tells me about a recent breakup.
- A father boasts in the challenges and rewards of family.
- A girl is proud of herself as she stares down her fear of flying.
- Someone explains steps that she is taking to improve her health.
- One man holds a little baby, recalling when his children were tiny.
- Someone cries when she surpasses a personal goal she has never reached before.

Some of my best times were when I randomly started chatting with people from the area, usually starting at the hotel. I have had conversations with staff, owners, and volunteers while I learned more about the area. If you give people a chance, they will reminisce about favorite locations, recommend parks and restaurants, and give pitfalls to avoid. A favorite moment from one new city visit was when I sat in a hotel lobby drinking local tea, talking with the owner about historical locations and where to eat dinner. When you sit down to have a conversation with a new friend, you build connections. You are no longer a complete stranger in the area, but have put a face to a name. Interactions like this build confidence as you explore and bring you face to face with each person's story. It is a simple, yet effective, way to say, "I see you." Who knows what impact that will have on the next person and then the next?

During our first visit to Amsterdam, my traveling companions and I met up with a friend for the day. She brought us to a favorite restaurant where we all tried to order something authentic and ended up with fried dishes. She showed us how to mix ketchup and mayonnaise with pepper as a condiment to dip our "chips" into. It might be a fairly normal practice, but it is a moment I remember because during that lunch trip, there was lots of laughter and new tastes tried. It was a time where we were becoming a part of the culture with little intention, but an authentic moment. You don't have to find a huge moment. Just keep your eyes open and embrace the time that you are given.

In conclusion:

- Find new friends in the activities that you choose.
- Learn from other people's ways of living.
- Change your outlook after your trip.
- When you get back from your trip, look back at the people who became your friends.
- Consider your encounters — The unexpected or difficult moments; the surprises and successes.

Chapter 7: History

One of the trips that I am extremely glad that I chose was riding a bus across Ireland from Dublin to the Cliffs of Moher, about a four hour journey. The guide was hilarious, throwing out jokes while explaining the landscape and the history that surrounded us as we drove. She would point out something and explain the legend where it might have originated, like how the sheep eating in the field became a black sheep. She recounted the entire story to the group with a straight face. As the day wore on, I could tell that she was extremely knowledgeable, but made the background of the area interesting. This is a great option if you have the money or inclination to hear about history as you are actually touring the area. It reminded me of the importance of storytelling to pass on traditions and creating moments that will stick with others so that they remember something important. You will be able to tell if it is a memory that will last, especially if it makes them laugh as they recall it many times over.

Appreciation

History can be as fun as solely discovering hidden gems in the nearest tiny town. The exploration doesn't have to be dry and it doesn't even need to include a textbook. Historical fiction books are my go-to, like *The DaVinci Code* (Brown) or *The Book Thief*

(Zusak) for places around Europe. I also love to find visual guides because I can observe what is being explained and they give tips on the side of the pages. A month before I visited New Zealand, I bought a small book that included brief information on the customs and cultures, and it was small enough to fit in my pocket or backpack for reference while I was traveling. More than the book, history is the story of real people and real cultures. It might just seem like a fairy tale as you listen to stories, but when you experience history as you explore, the hands-on involvement makes it increasingly more personal. I've included a *definitely not complete* list of my favorite books, mostly with a nod towards travel, in References. We have the advantage to look back at history now, but just by placing your feet on the soil as you study, you create your own history!

When you begin your investigation, you might stumble across an article the week you begin packing. A friend might mention favorite facts about a place because she's been there three times with her family. Don't roll your eyes (yes, I know you!). Jot down a few notes. Make a list of museums, coffee shops, or swimming holes. Design your own walking tour. A lot of prep work doesn't have to be designed in the beginning and yet, you can still learn.

Always find out the basic history of a place because it helps you appreciate what you are seeing with your own eyes. Instead of, "Oh, wow! That's a

gigantic rock! Let's take a picture next to it," you
would know that the stone is part of the original
foundation of a palace that is now in ruins. Or a
tunnel hidden in a hillside isn't just a hobbit hole, but
was a mine that was used for nearly fifty years, which
trapped miners during a horrific accident. One of the
great things about journeying to discover a new place
is that you are actually *there*. Stating the obvious here,
but physically putting yourself in the area is one
hundred times better than reading about it in a book.
Take that from someone who loves reading. You can
write things down, snap pictures, and build
connections. You are walking through history!

Hidden gems in an area are always top on my list,
but if you can find a good walking tour, it's almost
like a treasure hunt and it gives purpose in your
wandering. I recently went on a walking tour when I
visited Cusco, Peru, and I simply began by looking
things up on Pinterest. I searched for "Top things to
see before visiting Machu Picchu" and marked each
location on Google Maps as a new guide titled,
"Walking Cusco." As I researched, I added a few
more locations based on things I was interested in
and made sure to include a lunch stop for the way
back. Then when I pulled up Google Maps,
everything covered less than 1.5 miles from my hotel,
using the option that ordered the notable points by
distance. If you create your walking tour in this way,
you can create a circuit or move from nearest to

farthest, allowing time at the end of your tour to ruminate over what you observed!

I enjoy putting these together because they are personalized and I get to enjoy some of the obvious historical things while still being tailored to my own interests. This is a similar method that my friends and I organized our gallivanting in Europe the first time we visited. Another way to put together a walking tour is to find one where someone has already created a list with historical facts attached as you wander to each spot. I did a tour like this in Scotland and just had to arrive at a place and read information in the article before moving on to the next point.

Architecture

Slowly but surely, I have begun to appreciate architecture more through my drawings. Ideally, I take ten to fifteen minutes to sketch a place and will later go back to watercolor it. Sometimes, especially when I am moving through an area quickly, I will take several snapshots or record a video to return to later. At one time, one of my friends living in Germany shared what she was learning in school. I had grabbed another friend for this visit and the three of us were walking around Munich right after Christmas. Picture it: Snow. Warm beanie. Sauerkraut. Brisk wind. Cathedral. We had ducked into the nearby cathedral mainly to get out of the harsh wind, but found ourselves instead in a holy moment, a breath of awe where we had to stop and appreciate why this structure was built and how it related to us at that juncture. As we stood in the middle of a cathedral in Germany, my friend began to relate details of what she had learned in class, pointing out specific elements in the decoration that related back to history, people at that time, beliefs in that culture, and even mythology. It made a single structure come to life in my mind, and allowed me to immerse myself in what the craftspeople might have considered as they were building the enormous structure. We were all Americans in Europe, but we didn't want to allow this moment to pass without acknowledging that that wasn't the only thing that defined us. When investigating structures which have been standing for hundreds and thousands of years, you can almost hear stories radiating from the construction of the stones, design of the architecture, and style of that society. Take in the moment!

The advantage of going someplace multiple times is that you often notice things that you had not observed before. Often the people who have been in the town for a while know about their ancestors, and can even point you in a direction to study by sharing favorite haunts of theirs. Speaking of haunts, even though ghost tours sound like something created for kids, they offer a fun method to learn, filled with stories, a primary way that our brain retains new information. If you want to explore the history of a town, find a course to learn through storytelling. You will be much more apt to remember a love story on the steps of a cathedral than you will to memorize dates about the construction of a building. However, if you can tie dates with a story or a funny anecdote, you will quickly recall the fact while telling the story later.

Before I leave this short chapter, I want to emphasize that the history of a place is not about memorizing dates or even recognizing architectural styles. It is about remembering what was accomplished in that place. What battle was fought in this certain location and how did it affect the people at the time? What can you see in the manner that houses were built or the structure of the landscape? What hints of the past have been maintained in contemporary patterns and design and why do you think this was so important to keep them integrated in present-day life? What phrases are still used today that have roots in the challenges that were faced centuries ago? What wrongs were brushed under the rug and are only now coming to light?

Each of these questions dives a little deeper not only into how a city was shaped, but how it affects people and culture today. Once you establish your goal for research, you can then begin to consider how it makes a difference in your own life and what you can do in the future to share your findings with others. History does not need to be lost. You can be a voice for the next generation.

In conclusion:

- To learn about the history of a culture builds an appreciation of place.
- Find hidden locations in a city to raise your personal wow-factor.
- Figure out ways to explore by getting to know people in the town.
- Learn about where people have been before your feet touch the soil.

PISA,
ITALY

Chapter 8
PRACTICAL VS. PEACEFUL

Chapter 8: Practical vs. Peaceful

You can still travel safely even when you are alone. Granted, I have put myself into a couple of sticky situations, but for the most part, if you keep your eyes open, prepare to be smart, do not carry valuables in sight, and do not stupidly place yourself in situations that could put you in danger, you will come out on the other side. Yes, I have traveled on foot at night. Sometimes you can't help it because you are arriving late in a country or you are getting in from an excursion that took longer than you thought. Several places are known for being safe and having areas that welcome people at all moments of the night. In most places, you will have people to help you find your way. In Spain, for example, that city never sleeps. Sometimes you can find a friend who will show you new places and completely eliminate the worry that you would have walking by yourself.

Even as I write this, I realize I am painting a scary picture. It seems almost impossible for things to go right, so why try? Why would someone even want to put themselves in a situation that is so stressful? Wouldn't it be easier to stay home? Yes. Yes it would. But when you come out of this tunnel vision of fear, you can see the world. Meet new people. Try new things. Expand your view! Not just physically, but emotionally.

Figure out your personal beliefs. This is important because you will encounter some lovely people on your journey. They will tell you their stories, give advice, and even offer recommendations. You will also find those who grind on your nerves. You will need to process how you are going to reset when you are bothered and why you behaved in a certain way. This is easier said than done, but if you have already begun to process how you might react, it will help when actually responding to a situation.

Allow yourself to live a little. You are in another country so hopefully you will try new things. Some of this can be uncomfortable or embarrassing. Do not allow yourself to dwell on feeling guilty for not handling a situation correctly. If a day or two has passed and something still irks you, take a moment to consider: *What about that situation would I go back and change? What did I learn? How would I like to process this next time? What am I proud of?* I have asked myself these exact things. By this point in the conversation, I realize that I did not handle a situation as well as I would have liked. In some cases, I wish I would have just ignored the trigger in the first place. You know what? When you find yourself in this conversation, remember that you tried! You now have an experience under your belt that will help you make better decisions when navigating the future, even if it is a little painful. Later it will make a very good story.

Unexpected Twists

When traveling, you sometimes have to juggle somewhat bad and definitely worse cases, particularly with weather or money. When I was hiking on the Appalachian Trail with my dad, a horrible storm came up. We were pretty far from our next shelter stop, so we decided to duck and cover on the side of the Trail, hoping it would pass soon. We found a way to stay fairly dry by sitting on one tarp and using another for a screen, while covering our packs with our ponchos. But after an hour, I realized this was not going to be one of those quickly-passing storms and elected to make a run for it. We did this for the first couple of miles until we hit a mountain with giant rock stairs, too tall to sprint up. We were exhausted and soaked by the time we made it to our shelter.

The Appalachian Trail is a good way to save money, but it does not mean that it's free. More details on how to prepare and what to pack can be found in the A.T. section of Chapter Five, "United States Exploration". To prepare for the unexpected, you have to consider your pack and the essential items, food and water-filters, shelter options, and taxis as needed. A little bit of planning before setting out on a journey can help calm your nerves, such as keeping everything zipped in the same place or scheduling a pickup on a certain day. It does not mean that you will be ready for every situation, but you might surprise yourself and find a creative way to solve a problem because you did think of eventualities.

Embrace the Normal

When I was in New Zealand, I was about two hours early to check into my hotel. While I was there for a group event, we were on our own at the beginning of the trip as well as travel arrangements to and from the South Island, "Te Waipounamu". I went to a nearby park to sketch and discovered walking was a very normal part of the daily routine there. When I came back to the hotel reception area to take my bags up to my room, the receptionist and I started talking about how schools are now teaching the Maori language to students, and some street names have been changed to reflect the Maori culture. This can be seen in Hawaiian and Polynesian cultures as well.

Just a reminder: Always treat local people with respect! Of course, there will be times when a situation is frustrating or you are in a hurry, but it does no good to be rude to get what you want. You are in their country. Sometimes you must compromise some of the things you are used to in order to respect their beliefs. By asking questions out of curiosity about their own culture, you might develop a friend for life!

You never know where you will meet people or what inspiration it will provide. I don't take the time to relax as often as I need to, but when I do, it gives ample opportunity to people-watch. What a great way to build connections and learn about how people act on a daily basis! When I visited Peru last year, I stayed in a little apartment close to a few friends of mine. During the second week, I helped out with the kids' after school care and taught English. The director apologized that there wasn't more for me to do. I told her it was a privilege for me to be there during that time because I got to see the daily life of how they lived, without the pretense of needing to be entertained at all hours of the day. I am not sure I would have said that even two years before! Spending time in that town was a chance to relax and take advantage of walking each morning to the nearby town.

I love when I reach the moment in a stay where I get the chance to buy groceries or wash my clothes. It might be done differently from what I'm used to, but it reminds me that we all function in a similar way. These small "normalities" are also a reminder that no matter how hard I think a chore is, it is part of daily life for some people. I am very spoiled. Working among the culture forces me to consider those around me and what they experience on a daily basis. Just because I do something one way does not mean that is the only way to experience it.

Thoughts

As a side note, when you buy a book, drawing pad, or a notebook for those occasional down times, it gives you a chance to process the places you have seen on your adventures. You can surprise yourself by journaling or building a small scrapbook. For one hiking trip, I drew a timeline and doodles of each new town alongside my journal pages. It was perfect later for remembering where I was while writing about each encounter.

Seek out a restaurant or a coffee shop nearby and just sit in the culture for a moment. People-watch. Keep things slow. Allow time to go by without having the pressure of a schedule. This will be extremely challenging on one hand for some of you because we are all so used to having every hour of our day planned out. On the other hand, it is worth it because it will cause you to get out of your thinking brain and to savor the moment. You will make observations and listen to how others interact. This deliberate pause in your trip will help you to breathe and to take a moment to decide what you are going to do next. If you are joining a group at some point in your trip, you might be tempted to speak up a lot, to explain your opinion, or to share what you have seen. You will always get a chance to do this! But if you rush through everything, moving from place to place all the time, you will get exhausted more easily and will regret the fact that you didn't stop and observe more. Yes, I enjoyed the tower of Pisa, but it was because I decided to stop and take funny pictures with my friends, ignoring the fact that I was tired after several days of travel and having already visited a couple countries. It was a lot for my first big trip, and while I can say I've been there, I look forward to the slower adventures when I return.

>>Biking through the south of Spain.

>>Hiking in New Zealand.

>>Completing the Appalachian Trail on the east side of the United States.

>>Spending more time in Italy.

>>Walking on the Great Wall of China.

Many of my plans for the future are still dreams, but for now, I am learning to translate what

>>Biking through the south of Spain.
>>Hiking in New Zealand.
>> Completing the Appalachian Trail on the east side of the United States.
>> Spending more time in Italy.
>> Walking on the Great Wall of China.

I have learned from other countries into my daily life.
I get up in the morning and write forty-five minutes
to an hour. I make my own coffee most days or visit
one of my favorite coffee shops. I enjoy places that
have baristas or hosts who speak other languages
because they draw in more of the culture around the
area. I love fluffy cinnamon rolls and chai tea, so if a
coffee shop knows how to do this, I'm sold! I love
restaurants or cafes with culture, that have art on the
walls and lots of space with plenty of tables.

Don't always feel like you must have
something planned. I learned this the hard way on a
trip with my sister. I know, not solo, but the steps to
planning your own events, even if you travel with
someone, is the same as when you travel by yourself.
This conscious break is the hardest concept for me to
grasp because when I am in another country, of
course I want to say yes to all the opportunities! *When
am I ever going to do this again?* Sometimes this does
pay off, but often you are left with a rushed event that
exhausts you, taking a lot of sparkle out of the
moment. In one instance, I wanted to finish a walking
tour, but nearly missed a Broadway musical in
London, England because of poor time management.
I had in mind to show my sister the Tower Bridge, but
did not realize it was more than a mile from the
previous part of the walking tour. Then we had to get
back to our hotel to grab our outfits. We were directed
to the wrong side of the theater and arrived out of

breath, but only about five minutes late. There was a small television in the waiting area where we watched the first twenty minutes or so with the several other people who had arrived late. The last-minute scheduling of Mary Poppins was a great choice! The clash in plans, however, was a reminder to always give ourselves more time than we think to move from one location to another, especially in a city we do not know well.

The best way to alleviate stress on a trip is to slow down and do something enjoyable. I found this out in Scotland, taking an entire afternoon to shop, eat breakfast at a locally recommended and family-owned restaurant, and scarf down gelato. Edinburgh was the last stop that my sister and I had planned for our ten-day birthday excursion. We were on the hunt for some used bookstores and the owner of the restaurant directed us toward one. We had to wander for a bit and literally squeeze through a skinny hallway to pass through to the stacks in the back. There was not much rhyme or reason and I'm sure one could get lost in there for hours, finding armfuls of treasures. Allowing ourselves to be present in that moment was worth more than filling our last few afternoons with tours and explorations, even if that means another visit at another time.

In conclusion:

- Each country has its own challenges.
- Find new things to explore in each area.
- Add to your personal wanderlist.
- Discover peaceful moments in the middle of traveling to new places.
- Be prepared to travel, but enjoy each moment!

Chapter 9

MISSED OPPORTUNITIES

Chapter 9: Missed Opportunities

You can always learn from mistakes and dream about opportunities to redo them. However, I do not believe in regret, so this chapter will be short. What I mean by this is that I do my very best not to live with the regret of "Oh, I wish I had done that," or "I could have figured out how to do that differently." I acknowledge that I can change some things, and then go on to dream about others. It does no good to live in the past of what ifs. Figure out what you can learn from mistakes, and set goals to meet them next time. There is more fun in an adventure full of mistakes and laughter than there is in a trip of fighting because things are not going exactly right. Step into the fun! In this section I'd like to share with you some of the mistakes I have made and lessons I've learned.

I will do it wrong. I am human. After all, I personally have the tendency to figure something out, and if it doesn't quite work how I think it should, I shrug and decide, "Whatever." That works for me because I enjoy putting myself into new challenges. But if that is not your personality, find something that works for you. Some people might pack closer to 50 pounds (or 30 kilos) in their bag. You have a special routine at night or you always buy souvenirs in the country you visit. Don't feel like you have to change everything right away. Find what works for you. Eventually, though, when you grow accustomed to more travel, as I hope this guidebook prompts you, your routines might change and you will begin to simplify. It will be easier to travel just with basics, collecting pictures and stories as souvenirs. You will find moments to enjoy the sounds of the traffic without listening to headphones. Spend an evening reading, writing, or resting instead of watching TV. Eating a light dinner and sitting outside for a sunset.

> Find an alternate route. Go get a cup of coffee. Sit on a bench and people watch. Book yourself for the next flight and hang out with friends. Read a book or go shopping. Take a nap.

Some things like train and bus strikes are inevitable. I learned later that these strikes are usually scheduled, so it might be possible to plan around them in some way. I have never been able to figure it out. When my friends and I heard that our train was not going to be leaving as planned, we inquired as to whether the buses would be a good alternative. We were willing to spend more than twice the amount of time just to reach our destination. Those workers were also on strike, but for a shorter amount of time. Eventually we were able to start working our way south, but we missed nearly two full days in Rome.

Even though we were only in the city for a day plus a couple hours, we made the most of it. Our hostel was right next to the Sistine Chapel, but it was closed because of Mass. A man from the hostel explained that if we get tickets to both the Forum and the Colosseum, we could see the Forum first and skip the long line to the Colosseum. This was a great plan and it was extremely interesting. I am not sure I would have gone to see the Forum otherwise, and it was a good history lesson before going into the more popular Colosseum. We ate, watched the sunset at Michelangelo's Pier and observed a miniature version of the David statue. One of my goals the next time I visit Italy is to spend several days in Rome.

One of the situations I was not expecting was when my phone's battery failed in the middle of a subway platform late at night – *and* it was the moment that I needed to figure out how to get to my hostel. A kind passenger lent me their phone to use for a few minutes and I was able to find directions and the correct subway to grab. I now carry a battery pack or charger with me on trips.

A regret that I have (at this point) was not seeing the Great Wall. When I was in southern China, in the city of Yangshuo, it was a very long train ride to get over there and I would have had to skip five days of classes. I chose instead to go hiking with friends, climbing mountains and eating pizza. In lieu of traveling across the country, I doubled my classes for that week since it was near the end of my stay. In that time, I pushed my Mandarin further than I would have otherwise.

Instead of seeing something like this as missing out, why not look at it as an opportunity you have chosen? You did have the chance to go white water rafting, but chose to climb the mountain for a few hours instead. You had a choice between sitting on the beach relaxing or twirling in a meadow. You had the option to leave immediately for extra time or spend twenty extra minutes writing down your thoughts. Take a moment for pictures or go splash in the river. There is nothing wrong with any of these choices. It is the path you choose. And each answer that you say YES to doesn't mean that you miss out on the other. I read Robert Frost as a teenager and that poem about the "road not taken" is always in the back of my mind. But I recommend that you don't spend your entire life wondering what your other path would have been. Instead, create your own journey through your own choices. And if you keep coming back to the "I wish I would have…" then make a plan to go and do that! It can be your new adventure.

Don't miss out on the small opportunities. I read my Bible in the morning (mostly!) consistently. My wake-up routine includes Yoga With Adriene, which you can investigate more in the References. I drink coffee and write my morning pages. You can slide into small, "normal" things or even tweak what you have going to develop new morning habits. However you choose to use it, these miniscule acts will encourage you to have a good, positive mindset, no matter what the day holds. You will be more aware of what is going on around you and expectant of what will happen next. It's simple; maybe twenty to thirty minutes to start your day could seem irrelevant, but will make a big impact!

Circumstances will go awry. Your carefully laid plans will go wrong. I am by nature an optimist, especially when it comes to travel. "Put me in, Coach!" But with travel, something always goes wrong. And inevitably, the problem is not what you would expect. If you had expected it initially, you would have prepared for it. Your luggage will break, you won't be able to pull up your e-ticket. You'll take the wrong turn. Your flight will get delayed or the train will go on strike. You will read instructions wrong. But you know what? Find an alternate route. Go get a cup of coffee. Sit on a bench and people watch. Book yourself for the next flight and hang out with friends. Read a book or go shopping. Take a nap. It does NO good to get upset — let me rephrase that: to STAY upset. Face it. We're human and are going to get upset when things do not go right. By staying calm we are able to think more clearly and make rational decisions.

In conclusion:

- Don't let a few bad experiences ruin your outlook of a country.
  - Learn to listen to others and find out their stories.
- Shed light on new places that you wouldn't have previously considered.
  - Work through regrets by using travel as therapy.

Ready to Go?

As I was editing this book, I had the grand pleasure of working in Cusco, Peru. I have visited Peru several times, but this was the trip that I felt like it was becoming more natural to explore. I was still visiting places that I did not know, but it did not worry me because I was used to the environment and response of people on a daily basis. When I messed up with the language, I was not embarrassed, but rather tried to find alternate ways to communicate. Despite my protest against collecting unnecessary items, I did go a little overboard with souvenirs because I finally found a stacked ring that looked like the mountains I hiked in Peru. I bought a poncho because the early and late hours of the day were considerably colder than I was prepared for. Even though I acted like a tourist in some instances, I became more familiar in my interactions with those who lived in the country. I only hope that grows with every other visit!

Traveling solo does not always mean that you are going to travel alone. It might start out with a singular plan, but you will encounter people along the way who will help you. Some will challenge you. And some might even change your mind. You will learn more rapidly about adventure and taking advantage of each moment though listening and helping those around you, no matter what culture, religion, or country. Friends can be found everywhere.

There are different cultures no matter where you go. You could even drive an hour from your town right now to experience a different culture. Here is the key: Appreciate the culture. It might be weird at times, or downright scary, but what can you learn?

What strikes you first might be the weather. It is sticky and humid when you are used to living in a hot, dry environment. Or you are surrounded by trees when you are used to watching the sunset. You might find yourself in a busy city when

- You could have a mosquito infestation in your cabin and a party is going on across the street at 4:00 in the morning.
- You do not have enough blankets on your bed.
- You have to use the bathroom and can't find your shower shoes to walk to the outhouse or community bathrooms.
- You just stubbed your toe on someone's suitcase lying in the middle of the floor.

you are used to living by the sea. Whatever it is, find something to enjoy. You could have a mosquito infestation in your cabin and a party is going on across the street at 4:00 in the morning. You do not have enough blankets on your bed. You have to use the bathroom and can't find your shower shoes to walk to the outhouse or community bathrooms. You just stubbed your toe on someone's suitcase lying in the middle of the floor.

This is the moment that you blow up and scream "I hate it here!" (internally, of course, because waking up your flat mates in the hostel just isn't worth it). Now is the time that you find this courage within. This outside-the-box thinking you didn't know existed. Instead of getting frustrated, do what you can.

• You bury yourself under your sheets and even put a T-shirt on your head because sweating the rest of the night is far better than getting eaten by mosquitos.

• You put your headphones on full blast or get up to write a song to the beat of the obnoxious music.

• You make a list of what you would like to do the next day.

• You go to the bathroom in bare feet or socks. Gross? Yes, but not life-threatening, usually.

• You do twenty jumping jacks in the dark and make sure to put your beanie on under your hoodie. Maybe even shoes. Putting a pack on top of feet wouldn't be bad either.

Traveling alone will give you many opportunities to complain. When encountering other wanderers, the default method is to see who has the worst "war stories." But in the long run, it's just not worth it. Do you want to remember missing your train because you misread the instructions for how to reach the train platform? Or the fact that you ate an amazing gyro with chips? That you only had one day in Rome or that you got to check a couple places off your wanderlist? That you were dehydrated on your first two-hour bike ride in China? Or that you got to do it again with friends a week later? There will be many chances for things to go wrong when traveling. There are always too many variables and what-ifs in a journey. But if you allow uncertainty to keep you from getting out there, you are going to miss a lot.

I am a seven on the Enneagram, which is a nine-point personality test. This means that my worst fear is FOMO, the Fear Of Missing Out. I want to do all the things. I want to say yes to all the countries, all the cultures, all the experiences. But if I want to have a meaningful travel experience, I must learn to stop and breathe. To enjoy the moment. Watch that three-hour movie with my new language friends. Spend an extra hour to finish a serious conversation over noodles and soup. Get up early to go to my language tutor's favorite breakfast place. Take pictures on a ferry that I wasn't even supposed to have been on, thanks to delays. Sit in a coffee shop for an hour before heading to the airport. Drink horchata in a park for two hours chatting with a family member I have not seen in years. Say yes to karaoke. Try a new running path. Ask someone for directions.

Allow yourself to experience these things and to take notice! That will make any trip memorable.

Now get out there!

References

APPS

Airbnb	Renting rooms and houses for vacation
Duolingo	Basic Language Practice
Expedia	Hotels, flights, exploring
Far Out	Travel guides and interactive maps for Appalachian Trail
Google Translate	Basic language translation
Hostel World	Finding and booking hostels
Kayak	Hotels, flights, exploring
Pimsleur	Language communication practice
Pinterest	lists, pictures, and links
Rail Planner	Booking European train tickets
WeChat	Texting and calling app used in several countries
WhatsApp	Texting and calling app used in several countries

BOOKS

Languages
Read & Think French. McGraw-Hill Education, 2017.

Hsueh, ShaoLan, and Noma Bar. *Chineasy: The New Way to Read Chinese*. Harper Design, an Imprint of

HarperCollinsPublishers, 2014.

European Phrase Book. DK Publishing, 2003.

Spanish English Bilingual Visual Dictionary. DK Publishing, 2017.

Literature
Brown, Dan. *The Da Vinci Code: Special Illustrated Edition*. Doubleday, 2004.*

Cohen, Barbara, and Bahija Fattuhi Lovejoy. *Seven Daughters & Seven Sons*. Beech Tree Books, 1994.

Doerr, Anthony. *All the Light We Cannot See: A Novel*. Scribner, 2014.*

Frost, Robert, and Kenneth C. Mondschein. *A Collection of Poems by Robert Frost*. Printers Row Publishing Group, 2019.

Hannah, Kristin. *The Nightingale: A Novel*. St. Martin's Griffin, 2022.

Lang, Ruth Emmie, et al. *Beasts of Extraordinary Circumstance: A Novel*. HighBridge, 2017.

Leaf, Caroline. *Switch on Your Brain: The Key to Peak Happiness, Thinking, and Health*. BakerBooks, a Division of Baker Publishing Group, 2015.

Locke, Tembi. *From Scratch: A Memoir of Love, Sicily, and Finding Home*. Simon & Schuster; Reprint Edition, 2020.*

Martin, Charles. *The Mountain Between Us: A Novel.* Crown, 2010.*

McCord, Kate. *In the Land of the Blue Burqas.* Moody Press, 2012.

Sepetys, Ruta. *The Fountains of Silence: A Novel.* Philomel Books, 2020.*

Shaffer, Mary Ann, and Annie Barrows. *The Guernsey Literary and Potato Peel Pie Society.* Bloomsbury Publishing, 2019.*

Stanton, Brandon. *Humans.* St. Martin's Press, an Imprint of St. Martin's Publishing Group, 2020.

Zusak, Markus. *The Book Thief.* Black Swan, 2014.*

Travel

Butler, Susan. *Culture Smart: New Zealand.* Kuperard ; Distributed in the United States and Canada by Random House Distribution Services, 2006.

Cage, Chris. *How to Hike the Appalachian Trail: A Comprehensive Guide to Plan and Prepare for a Successful Thru-Hike.* Chris Cage, 2017.

Fitzgerald, Emma. *Hand-Drawn in Halifax: Portraits of the City's Buildings, Landmarks, Neighbourhoods and Residents.* 2nd ed., Formac, 2017.

Ilgunas, Ken. *Trespassing Across America: One Man's Epic, Never-Done-Before (and Sort of Illegal) Hike Across the Heartland.* Blue Rider Press, 2017.

McDougall, Christopher. *Born to Run a Hidden Tribe, Superathletes, and the Greatest Race the World Has Never Seen*. Random House, 2011.

Sanders, Ella Frances. *Lost in Translation: An Illustrated Compendium of Untranslatable Words from around the World*. Square Peg, 2015.

Oxenreider, Tsh. *At Home in the World: Reflections on Belonging While Wandering the Globe*. Thomas Nelson Publishers, 2017.

MENTIONS

"Find Your Voice." *Allison Fallon*, 29 Sept. 2022, allisonfallon.com/.

Hardy, Thomas. *Far from the Madding Crowd*. Oxford University Press, 2008.

"International Travel Documents for Children." *USAGov*, 6 Dec. 2023, www.usa.gov/travel-documents-children.

Mishler, Adriene. *Yoga With Adriene*, YouTube, 2024, www.youtube.com/user/yogawithadriene.

Montgomery, L. M. *Anne of Green Gables*. Grosset & Dunlap, 2001.

"Red Cross Training: Take A Class." *American Red Cross: Training Services*, 2024, www.redcross.org/take-a-class?utm_source=RCO&ut

m_medium=RCO_Navigation_Training_Certification.

"solivagant." *Merriam-Webster.com*. Merriam-Webster, Incorporated, 2024. Web. May 2024.

Travel.State.Gov , 2024, travel.state.gov/content/travel.html.

Ureta Hotel in Peru; Calle Lima C-12, Av. Collasuyo 521, Cusco 08003

Vacation Races, 4 June 2024, www.vacationraces.com/.

RESTAURANTS

Amsterdam, Netherlands	Anne and Max's
Coffee	
Shop	
Bethlehem, Pennsylvania, USA	Anna's Brick
Oven Pizza	
Cusco, Peru	Cicciolina Café
Edinburgh, Scotland	L'étoile: Salon de Thé
Europe	gelato - find at any
stand	
(favorite: nueces de mantequilla)	
Glasgow, Virginia, USA	Scotto's Italian Food
London, England	Nando's
PERi-PERi	
Munich, Germany	Cherry cart
seller	
Paris, France	Crepe Cart next

to the
Eiffel Tower
Plainview, Texas, USA   The Broadway Brew
Toronto, Canada   Glory Hole Donuts
Venice, Italy   Rossopomodoro
Washington, D.C., USA   Hill Country Barbecue
Market

*also found in several other languages

www.ingramcontent.com/pod-product-compliance
Lightning Source LLC
Chambersburg PA
CBHW051522120626

46551CB00012B/1041